Entry 1

📅 Date:			🌥 Weather Conditions:		
🕐 Time started:			☀ ⛅ 🌧 ⛈ 🌨		
🕐 Time finished:			○ ○ ○ ○ ○		
💡 Skills Practiced:			📍 Type of Driving (Rural,City,Highway. etc):		

Day Minutes:		Night Minutes:		Total Minutes:	
Carried Forward:		Carried Forward:		Carried Forward:	
Total To Date:		Total To Date:		Total To Date:	

📝 Notes:	👤 Instructor:
	🖊 Instructor's Signature:

Entry 2

📅 Date:			🌥 Weather Conditions:		
🕐 Time started:			☀ ⛅ 🌧 ⛈ 🌨		
🕐 Time finished:			○ ○ ○ ○ ○		
💡 Skills Practiced:			📍 Type of Driving (Rural,City,Highway. etc):		

Day Minutes:		Night Minutes:		Total Minutes:	
Carried Forward:		Carried Forward:		Carried Forward:	
Total To Date:		Total To Date:		Total To Date:	

📝 Notes:	👤 Instructor:
	🖊 Instructor's Signature:

Entry 1

📅 Date:

🕐 Time started:

🕐 Time finished:

💡 Skills Practiced:

☁ Weather Conditions:

☀ ⛅ 🌧 ⛈ 🌦
○ ○ ○ ○ ○

📍 Type of Driving (Rural,City,Highway. etc):

Day Minutes:		Night Minutes:			Total Minutes:	
Carried Forward:		Carried Forward:			Carried Forward:	
Total To Date:		Total To Date:			Total To Date:	

📝 Notes:

👤 Instructor:

✍ Instructor's Signature:

Entry 2

📅 Date:

🕐 Time started:

🕐 Time finished:

💡 Skills Practiced:

☁ Weather Conditions:

☀ ⛅ 🌧 ⛈ 🌦
○ ○ ○ ○ ○

📍 Type of Driving (Rural,City,Highway. etc):

Day Minutes:		Night Minutes:			Total Minutes:	
Carried Forward:		Carried Forward:			Carried Forward:	
Total To Date:		Total To Date:			Total To Date:	

📝 Notes:

👤 Instructor:

✍ Instructor's Signature:

Entry 1

📅 Date:		☁ Weather Conditions:
🕐 Time started:		☀ ⛅ 🌧 ⛈ 🌧
🕐 Time finished:		○ ○ ○ ○ ○

💡 Skills Practiced:

📍 Type of Driving (Rural,City,Highway. etc):

Day Minutes:		Night Minutes:			Total Minutes:	
Carried Forward:		Carried Forward:			Carried Forward:	
Total To Date:		Total To Date:			Total To Date:	

📝 Notes:

👤 Instructor:

🖊 Instructor's Signature:

Entry 2

📅 Date:		☁ Weather Conditions:
🕐 Time started:		☀ ⛅ 🌧 ⛈ 🌧
🕐 Time finished:		○ ○ ○ ○ ○

💡 Skills Practiced:

📍 Type of Driving (Rural,City,Highway. etc):

Day Minutes:		Night Minutes:			Total Minutes:	
Carried Forward:		Carried Forward:			Carried Forward:	
Total To Date:		Total To Date:			Total To Date:	

📝 Notes:

👤 Instructor:

🖊 Instructor's Signature:

Entry 1

📅 Date:

🕐 Time started:

🕐 Time finished:

💡 Skills Practiced:

☁ Weather Conditions:

☀ ⛅ 🌧 ⛈ 🌨
○ ○ ○ ○ ○

📍 Type of Driving (Rural, City, Highway. etc):

Day Minutes:		Night Minutes:		Total Minutes:	
Carried Forward:		Carried Forward:		Carried Forward:	
Total To Date:		Total To Date:		Total To Date:	

📝 Notes:

👤 Instructor:

🖊 Instructor's Signature:

Entry 2

📅 Date:

🕐 Time started:

🕐 Time finished:

💡 Skills Practiced:

☁ Weather Conditions:

☀ ⛅ 🌧 ⛈ 🌨
○ ○ ○ ○ ○

📍 Type of Driving (Rural, City, Highway. etc):

Day Minutes:		Night Minutes:		Total Minutes:	
Carried Forward:		Carried Forward:		Carried Forward:	
Total To Date:		Total To Date:		Total To Date:	

📝 Notes:

👤 Instructor:

🖊 Instructor's Signature:

📅 Date:		☁ Weather Conditions:		
🕐 Time started:		☀ ⛅ 🌧 ⛈ 🌨		
🕐 Time finished:		○ ○ ○ ○ ○		
💡 Skills Practiced:		📍 Type of Driving (Rural,City,Highway. etc):		

Day Minutes:		Night Minutes:		Total Minutes:	
Carried Forward:		Carried Forward:		Carried Forward:	
Total To Date:		Total To Date:		Total To Date:	

📝 Notes:	👤 Instructor:
	✍ Instructor's Signature:

📅 Date:		☁ Weather Conditions:		
🕐 Time started:		☀ ⛅ 🌧 ⛈ 🌨		
🕐 Time finished:		○ ○ ○ ○ ○		
💡 Skills Practiced:		📍 Type of Driving (Rural,City,Highway. etc):		

Day Minutes:		Night Minutes:		Total Minutes:	
Carried Forward:		Carried Forward:		Carried Forward:	
Total To Date:		Total To Date:		Total To Date:	

📝 Notes:	👤 Instructor:
	✍ Instructor's Signature:

Entry 1

📅 Date:

🕐 Time started:

🕐 Time finished:

💡 Skills Practiced:

☁ Weather Conditions:

☀ ⛅ 🌧 ⛈ 🌨
○　○　○　○　○

📍 Type of Driving (Rural,City,Highway. etc):

Day Minutes:		Night Minutes:			Total Minutes:	
Carried Forward:		Carried Forward:			Carried Forward:	
Total To Date:		Total To Date:			Total To Date:	

📝 Notes:

👤 Instructor:

🖊 Instructor's Signature:

Entry 2

📅 Date:

🕐 Time started:

🕐 Time finished:

💡 Skills Practiced:

☁ Weather Conditions:

☀ ⛅ 🌧 ⛈ 🌨
○　○　○　○　○

📍 Type of Driving (Rural,City,Highway. etc):

Day Minutes:		Night Minutes:			Total Minutes:	
Carried Forward:		Carried Forward:			Carried Forward:	
Total To Date:		Total To Date:			Total To Date:	

📝 Notes:

👤 Instructor:

🖊 Instructor's Signature:

📅 Date:		☁ Weather Conditions:

🕐 Time started:

🕐 Time finished:

| ☀ ◯ | ⛅ ◯ | 🌧 ◯ | ⛈ ◯ | 🌨 ◯ |

🔆 Skills Practiced:

📍 Type of Driving (Rural,City,Highway. etc):

Day Minutes:		Night Minutes:		Total Minutes:	
Carried Forward:		Carried Forward:		Carried Forward:	
Total To Date:		Total To Date:		Total To Date:	

📝 Notes:

👤 Instructor:

✍ Instructor's Signature:

📅 Date:		☁ Weather Conditions:

🕐 Time started:

🕐 Time finished:

| ☀ ◯ | ⛅ ◯ | 🌧 ◯ | ⛈ ◯ | 🌨 ◯ |

🔆 Skills Practiced:

📍 Type of Driving (Rural,City,Highway. etc):

Day Minutes:		Night Minutes:		Total Minutes:	
Carried Forward:		Carried Forward:		Carried Forward:	
Total To Date:		Total To Date:		Total To Date:	

📝 Notes:

👤 Instructor:

✍ Instructor's Signature:

Entry 1

📅 Date:	☁ Weather Conditions:
🕐 Time started:	
🕐 Time finished:	☀ ⛅ 🌧 ⛈ 🌨
	○ ○ ○ ○ ○
🔆 Skills Practiced:	📍 Type of Driving (Rural,City,Highway. etc):

Day Minutes:		Night Minutes:			Total Minutes:	
Carried Forward:		Carried Forward:			Carried Forward:	
Total To Date:		Total To Date:			Total To Date:	

📝 Notes:	👤 Instructor:
	✒ Instructor's Signature:

Entry 2

📅 Date:	☁ Weather Conditions:
🕐 Time started:	
🕐 Time finished:	☀ ⛅ 🌧 ⛈ 🌨
	○ ○ ○ ○ ○
🔆 Skills Practiced:	📍 Type of Driving (Rural,City,Highway. etc):

Day Minutes:		Night Minutes:			Total Minutes:	
Carried Forward:		Carried Forward:			Carried Forward:	
Total To Date:		Total To Date:			Total To Date:	

📝 Notes:	👤 Instructor:
	✒ Instructor's Signature:

Entry 1

📅 Date:

🕐 Time started:

🕐 Time finished:

💡 Skills Practiced:

☁ Weather Conditions:

☀ ⛅ 🌧 ⛈ 🌨
○   ○   ○   ○   ○

📍 Type of Driving (Rural,City,Highway. etc):

Day Minutes:		Night Minutes:		Total Minutes:	
Carried Forward:		Carried Forward:		Carried Forward:	
Total To Date:		Total To Date:		Total To Date:	

📝 Notes:

👤 Instructor:

🖊 Instructor's Signature:

Entry 2

📅 Date:

🕐 Time started:

🕐 Time finished:

💡 Skills Practiced:

☁ Weather Conditions:

☀ ⛅ 🌧 ⛈ 🌨
○   ○   ○   ○   ○

📍 Type of Driving (Rural,City,Highway. etc):

Day Minutes:		Night Minutes:		Total Minutes:	
Carried Forward:		Carried Forward:		Carried Forward:	
Total To Date:		Total To Date:		Total To Date:	

📝 Notes:

👤 Instructor:

🖊 Instructor's Signature:

📅 Date:	☁ Weather Conditions:

🕐 Time started:	☀ ⛅ 🌧 ⛈ 🌨
🕐 Time finished:	○ ○ ○ ○ ○

💡 Skills Practiced:	📍 Type of Driving (Rural,City,Highway. etc):

Day Minutes:		Night Minutes:		Total Minutes:	
Carried Forward:		Carried Forward:		Carried Forward:	
Total To Date:		Total To Date:		Total To Date:	

📝 Notes:	👤 Instructor:
	✒ Instructor's Signature:

📅 Date:	☁ Weather Conditions:

🕐 Time started:	☀ ⛅ 🌧 ⛈ 🌨
🕐 Time finished:	○ ○ ○ ○ ○

💡 Skills Practiced:	📍 Type of Driving (Rural,City,Highway. etc):

Day Minutes:		Night Minutes:		Total Minutes:	
Carried Forward:		Carried Forward:		Carried Forward:	
Total To Date:		Total To Date:		Total To Date:	

📝 Notes:	👤 Instructor:
	✒ Instructor's Signature:

📅 Date:		☁ Weather Conditions:

🕐 Time started:

🕐 Time finished:

☀ 🌤 🌧 ⛈ 🌦
○ ○ ○ ○ ○

💡 Skills Practiced:

📍 Type of Driving (Rural,City,Highway. etc):

Day Minutes:		Night Minutes:		Total Minutes:	
Carried Forward:		Carried Forward:		Carried Forward:	
Total To Date:		Total To Date:		Total To Date:	

📝 Notes:

👤 Instructor:

🖊 Instructor's Signature:

📅 Date:		☁ Weather Conditions:

🕐 Time started:

🕐 Time finished:

☀ 🌤 🌧 ⛈ 🌦
○ ○ ○ ○ ○

💡 Skills Practiced:

📍 Type of Driving (Rural,City,Highway. etc):

Day Minutes:		Night Minutes:		Total Minutes:	
Carried Forward:		Carried Forward:		Carried Forward:	
Total To Date:		Total To Date:		Total To Date:	

📝 Notes:

👤 Instructor:

🖊 Instructor's Signature:

📅 Date:	☁ Weather Conditions:
🕐 Time started:	☀ ⛅ 🌧 ⛈ 🌨
🕐 Time finished:	○ ○ ○ ○ ○
💡 Skills Practiced:	📍 Type of Driving (Rural,City,Highway. etc):

Day Minutes:		Night Minutes:		Total Minutes:	
Carried Forward:		Carried Forward:		Carried Forward:	
Total To Date:		Total To Date:		Total To Date:	

📝 Notes:	👤 Instructor:
	✒ Instructor's Signature:

📅 Date:	☁ Weather Conditions:
🕐 Time started:	☀ ⛅ 🌧 ⛈ 🌨
🕐 Time finished:	○ ○ ○ ○ ○
💡 Skills Practiced:	📍 Type of Driving (Rural,City,Highway. etc):

Day Minutes:		Night Minutes:		Total Minutes:	
Carried Forward:		Carried Forward:		Carried Forward:	
Total To Date:		Total To Date:		Total To Date:	

📝 Notes:	👤 Instructor:
	✒ Instructor's Signature:

Entry 1

📅 Date:	☁ Weather Conditions:
🕐 Time started:	☀ ⛅ 🌧 ⛈ 🌦
🕐 Time finished:	○ ○ ○ ○ ○
💡 Skills Practiced:	📍 Type of Driving (Rural,City,Highway. etc):

Day Minutes:		Night Minutes:		Total Minutes:	
Carried Forward:		Carried Forward:		Carried Forward:	
Total To Date:		Total To Date:		Total To Date:	

📝 Notes:	👤 Instructor:
	✒ Instructor's Signature:

Entry 2

📅 Date:	☁ Weather Conditions:
🕐 Time started:	☀ ⛅ 🌧 ⛈ 🌦
🕐 Time finished:	○ ○ ○ ○ ○
💡 Skills Practiced:	📍 Type of Driving (Rural,City,Highway. etc):

Day Minutes:		Night Minutes:		Total Minutes:	
Carried Forward:		Carried Forward:		Carried Forward:	
Total To Date:		Total To Date:		Total To Date:	

📝 Notes:	👤 Instructor:
	✒ Instructor's Signature:

Date:

Time started:

Time finished:

Skills Practiced:

Weather Conditions:

☀ ⛅ 🌧 ⛈ 🌨
○ ○ ○ ○ ○

Type of Driving (Rural,City,Highway. etc):

Day Minutes:		Night Minutes:		Total Minutes:	
Carried Forward:		Carried Forward:		Carried Forward:	
Total To Date:		Total To Date:		Total To Date:	

Notes:

Instructor:

Instructor's Signature:

Date:

Time started:

Time finished:

Skills Practiced:

Weather Conditions:

☀ ⛅ 🌧 ⛈ 🌨
○ ○ ○ ○ ○

Type of Driving (Rural,City,Highway. etc):

Day Minutes:		Night Minutes:		Total Minutes:	
Carried Forward:		Carried Forward:		Carried Forward:	
Total To Date:		Total To Date:		Total To Date:	

Notes:

Instructor:

Instructor's Signature:

Entry 1

📅 Date:

🕐 Time started:

🕐 Time finished:

💡 Skills Practiced:

☁ Weather Conditions:

☀ ⛅ 🌧 ⛈ 🌦
○ ○ ○ ○ ○

📍 Type of Driving (Rural,City,Highway. etc):

Day Minutes:		Night Minutes:		Total Minutes:	
Carried Forward:		Carried Forward:		Carried Forward:	
Total To Date:		Total To Date:		Total To Date:	

📝 Notes:

👤 Instructor:

🖋 Instructor's Signature:

Entry 2

📅 Date:

🕐 Time started:

🕐 Time finished:

💡 Skills Practiced:

☁ Weather Conditions:

☀ ⛅ 🌧 ⛈ 🌦
○ ○ ○ ○ ○

📍 Type of Driving (Rural,City,Highway. etc):

Day Minutes:		Night Minutes:		Total Minutes:	
Carried Forward:		Carried Forward:		Carried Forward:	
Total To Date:		Total To Date:		Total To Date:	

📝 Notes:

👤 Instructor:

🖋 Instructor's Signature:

Entry 1

📅 Date:	☁ Weather Conditions:
🕐 Time started:	☀ ⛅ 🌧 ⛈ 🌨
🕐 Time finished:	○ ○ ○ ○ ○
💡 Skills Practiced:	📍 Type of Driving (Rural,City,Highway. etc):

Day Minutes:		Night Minutes:			Total Minutes:	
Carried Forward:		Carried Forward:			Carried Forward:	
Total To Date:		Total To Date:			Total To Date:	

📝 Notes:	👤 Instructor:
	✍ Instructor's Signature:

Entry 2

📅 Date:	☁ Weather Conditions:
🕐 Time started:	☀ ⛅ 🌧 ⛈ 🌨
🕐 Time finished:	○ ○ ○ ○ ○
💡 Skills Practiced:	📍 Type of Driving (Rural,City,Highway. etc):

Day Minutes:		Night Minutes:			Total Minutes:	
Carried Forward:		Carried Forward:			Carried Forward:	
Total To Date:		Total To Date:			Total To Date:	

📝 Notes:	👤 Instructor:
	✍ Instructor's Signature:

Entry 1

📅 Date:		🌥 Weather Conditions:
🕐 Time started:		
🕐 Time finished:		☀️ ⛅ 🌧 ⛈ 🌨
		○ ○ ○ ○ ○

💡 Skills Practiced:

📍 Type of Driving (Rural,City,Highway. etc):

Day Minutes:		Night Minutes:		Total Minutes:	
Carried Forward:		Carried Forward:		Carried Forward:	
Total To Date:		Total To Date:		Total To Date:	

📝 Notes:

👤 Instructor:

✒️ Instructor's Signature:

Entry 2

📅 Date:		🌥 Weather Conditions:
🕐 Time started:		
🕐 Time finished:		☀️ ⛅ 🌧 ⛈ 🌨
		○ ○ ○ ○ ○

💡 Skills Practiced:

📍 Type of Driving (Rural,City,Highway. etc):

Day Minutes:		Night Minutes:		Total Minutes:	
Carried Forward:		Carried Forward:		Carried Forward:	
Total To Date:		Total To Date:		Total To Date:	

📝 Notes:

👤 Instructor:

✒️ Instructor's Signature:

Entry 1

Date:

Time started:

Time finished:

Skills Practiced:

Weather Conditions:

☀ ⛅ 🌧 ⛈ 🌦
○　○　○　○　○

Type of Driving (Rural,City,Highway. etc):

Day Minutes:		Night Minutes:		Total Minutes:	
Carried Forward:		Carried Forward:		Carried Forward:	
Total To Date:		Total To Date:		Total To Date:	

Notes:

Instructor:

Instructor's Signature:

Entry 2

Date:

Time started:

Time finished:

Skills Practiced:

Weather Conditions:

☀ ⛅ 🌧 ⛈ 🌦
○　○　○　○　○

Type of Driving (Rural,City,Highway. etc):

Day Minutes:		Night Minutes:		Total Minutes:	
Carried Forward:		Carried Forward:		Carried Forward:	
Total To Date:		Total To Date:		Total To Date:	

Notes:

Instructor:

Instructor's Signature:

Entry 1

📅 Date:		☁ Weather Conditions:

🕐 Time started:
🕐 Time finished:

☀ ⛅ 🌦 ⛈ 🌧
○ ○ ○ ○ ○

💡 Skills Practiced:

📍 Type of Driving (Rural,City,Highway. etc):

Day Minutes:		Night Minutes:		Total Minutes:	
Carried Forward:		Carried Forward:		Carried Forward:	
Total To Date:		Total To Date:		Total To Date:	

📝 Notes:

👤 Instructor:

🖊 Instructor's Signature:

Entry 2

📅 Date:		☁ Weather Conditions:

🕐 Time started:
🕐 Time finished:

☀ ⛅ 🌦 ⛈ 🌧
○ ○ ○ ○ ○

💡 Skills Practiced:

📍 Type of Driving (Rural,City,Highway. etc):

Day Minutes:		Night Minutes:		Total Minutes:	
Carried Forward:		Carried Forward:		Carried Forward:	
Total To Date:		Total To Date:		Total To Date:	

📝 Notes:

👤 Instructor:

🖊 Instructor's Signature:

Entry 1

Date:	Weather Conditions:
Time started:	☀ ⛅ 🌧 ⛈ 🌨
Time finished:	○ ○ ○ ○ ○
Skills Practiced:	Type of Driving (Rural,City,Highway. etc):

Day Minutes:		Night Minutes:		Total Minutes:	
Carried Forward:		Carried Forward:		Carried Forward:	
Total To Date:		Total To Date:		Total To Date:	

Notes:	Instructor:
	Instructor's Signature:

Entry 2

Date:	Weather Conditions:
Time started:	☀ ⛅ 🌧 ⛈ 🌨
Time finished:	○ ○ ○ ○ ○
Skills Practiced:	Type of Driving (Rural,City,Highway. etc):

Day Minutes:		Night Minutes:		Total Minutes:	
Carried Forward:		Carried Forward:		Carried Forward:	
Total To Date:		Total To Date:		Total To Date:	

Notes:	Instructor:
	Instructor's Signature:

Entry 1

📅 Date:		Weather Conditions:
🕐 Time started:		☀ ⛅ 🌧 ⛈ 🌨
🕐 Time finished:		○ ○ ○ ○ ○

🔆 Skills Practiced:

📍 Type of Driving (Rural, City, Highway. etc):

Day Minutes:		Night Minutes:			Total Minutes:	
Carried Forward:		Carried Forward:			Carried Forward:	
Total To Date:		Total To Date:			Total To Date:	

📝 Notes:

👤 Instructor:

✍ Instructor's Signature:

Entry 2

📅 Date:		Weather Conditions:
🕐 Time started:		☀ ⛅ 🌧 ⛈ 🌨
🕐 Time finished:		○ ○ ○ ○ ○

🔆 Skills Practiced:

📍 Type of Driving (Rural, City, Highway. etc):

Day Minutes:		Night Minutes:			Total Minutes:	
Carried Forward:		Carried Forward:			Carried Forward:	
Total To Date:		Total To Date:			Total To Date:	

📝 Notes:

👤 Instructor:

✍ Instructor's Signature:

Entry 1

📅 Date:			🌥 Weather Conditions:		
🕐 Time started:			☀ 🌤 🌧 ⛈ 🌨		
🕐 Time finished:			○ ○ ○ ○ ○		
💡 Skills Practiced:			📍 Type of Driving (Rural,City,Highway. etc):		

Day Minutes:		Night Minutes:		Total Minutes:	
Carried Forward:		Carried Forward:		Carried Forward:	
Total To Date:		Total To Date:		Total To Date:	

📝 Notes:	👤 Instructor:
	✍ Instructor's Signature:

Entry 2

📅 Date:			🌥 Weather Conditions:		
🕐 Time started:			☀ 🌤 🌧 ⛈ 🌨		
🕐 Time finished:			○ ○ ○ ○ ○		
💡 Skills Practiced:			📍 Type of Driving (Rural,City,Highway. etc):		

Day Minutes:		Night Minutes:		Total Minutes:	
Carried Forward:		Carried Forward:		Carried Forward:	
Total To Date:		Total To Date:		Total To Date:	

📝 Notes:	👤 Instructor:
	✍ Instructor's Signature:

Entry 1

📅 Date:

🕐 Time started:

🕐 Time finished:

💡 Skills Practiced:

☁ Weather Conditions:

☀ ⛅ 🌧 ⛈ 🌧
○ ○ ○ ○ ○

📍 Type of Driving (Rural,City,Highway. etc):

Day Minutes:		Night Minutes:			Total Minutes:	
Carried Forward:		Carried Forward:			Carried Forward:	
Total To Date:		Total To Date:			Total To Date:	

📝 Notes:

👤 Instructor:

🖊 Instructor's Signature:

Entry 2

📅 Date:

🕐 Time started:

🕐 Time finished:

💡 Skills Practiced:

☁ Weather Conditions:

☀ ⛅ 🌧 ⛈ 🌧
○ ○ ○ ○ ○

📍 Type of Driving (Rural,City,Highway. etc):

Day Minutes:		Night Minutes:			Total Minutes:	
Carried Forward:		Carried Forward:			Carried Forward:	
Total To Date:		Total To Date:			Total To Date:	

📝 Notes:

👤 Instructor:

🖊 Instructor's Signature:

Entry 1

📅 Date:		☁ Weather Conditions:	
🕐 Time started:		☀ ⛅ 🌧 ⛈ 🌨	
🕐 Time finished:		○ ○ ○ ○ ○	
💡 Skills Practiced:		📍 Type of Driving (Rural,City,Highway. etc):	

Day Minutes:		Night Minutes:		Total Minutes:	
Carried Forward:		Carried Forward:		Carried Forward:	
Total To Date:		Total To Date:		Total To Date:	

📝 Notes:	👤 Instructor:
	✒ Instructor's Signature:

Entry 2

📅 Date:		☁ Weather Conditions:	
🕐 Time started:		☀ ⛅ 🌧 ⛈ 🌨	
🕐 Time finished:		○ ○ ○ ○ ○	
💡 Skills Practiced:		📍 Type of Driving (Rural,City,Highway. etc):	

Day Minutes:		Night Minutes:		Total Minutes:	
Carried Forward:		Carried Forward:		Carried Forward:	
Total To Date:		Total To Date:		Total To Date:	

📝 Notes:	👤 Instructor:
	✒ Instructor's Signature:

Date:		Weather Conditions:

☀ ○ ⛅ ○ 🌧 ○ ⛈ ○ 🌦 ○

🕐 Time started:	
🕐 Time finished:	

💡 Skills Practiced:	📍 Type of Driving (Rural,City,Highway. etc):

Day Minutes:		Night Minutes:		Total Minutes:	
Carried Forward:		Carried Forward:		Carried Forward:	
Total To Date:		Total To Date:		Total To Date:	

📝 Notes:	👤 Instructor:
	✍ Instructor's Signature:

Date:		Weather Conditions:

☀ ○ ⛅ ○ 🌧 ○ ⛈ ○ 🌦 ○

🕐 Time started:	
🕐 Time finished:	

💡 Skills Practiced:	📍 Type of Driving (Rural,City,Highway. etc):

Day Minutes:		Night Minutes:		Total Minutes:	
Carried Forward:		Carried Forward:		Carried Forward:	
Total To Date:		Total To Date:		Total To Date:	

📝 Notes:	👤 Instructor:
	✍ Instructor's Signature:

Entry 1

Date:		Weather Conditions:

Time started:

Time finished:

Skills Practiced:

Type of Driving (Rural,City,Highway. etc):

Day Minutes:		Night Minutes:			Total Minutes:	
Carried Forward:		Carried Forward:			Carried Forward:	
Total To Date:		Total To Date:			Total To Date:	

Notes:

Instructor:

Instructor's Signature:

Entry 2

Date:		Weather Conditions:

Time started:

Time finished:

Skills Practiced:

Type of Driving (Rural,City,Highway. etc):

Day Minutes:		Night Minutes:			Total Minutes:	
Carried Forward:		Carried Forward:			Carried Forward:	
Total To Date:		Total To Date:			Total To Date:	

Notes:

Instructor:

Instructor's Signature:

Entry 1

📅 Date:				
🕐 Time started:		☁ Weather Conditions:		
🕐 Time finished:		☀ ⛅ 🌧 ⛈ 🌨 ○ ○ ○ ○ ○		

💡 Skills Practiced:

📍 Type of Driving (Rural,City,Highway. etc):

Day Minutes:		Night Minutes:		Total Minutes:	
Carried Forward:		Carried Forward:		Carried Forward:	
Total To Date:		Total To Date:		Total To Date:	

📝 Notes:

👤 Instructor:

✒ Instructor's Signature:

Entry 2

📅 Date:				
🕐 Time started:		☁ Weather Conditions:		
🕐 Time finished:		☀ ⛅ 🌧 ⛈ 🌨 ○ ○ ○ ○ ○		

💡 Skills Practiced:

📍 Type of Driving (Rural,City,Highway. etc):

Day Minutes:		Night Minutes:		Total Minutes:	
Carried Forward:		Carried Forward:		Carried Forward:	
Total To Date:		Total To Date:		Total To Date:	

📝 Notes:

👤 Instructor:

✒ Instructor's Signature:

Date:	Weather Conditions:
Time started:	☀ ⛅ 🌦 ⛈ 🌧
Time finished:	○ ○ ○ ○ ○
Skills Practiced:	Type of Driving (Rural,City,Highway. etc):

Day Minutes:		Night Minutes:		Total Minutes:	
Carried Forward:		Carried Forward:		Carried Forward:	
Total To Date:		Total To Date:		Total To Date:	

Notes:	Instructor:
	Instructor's Signature:

Date:	Weather Conditions:
Time started:	☀ ⛅ 🌦 ⛈ 🌧
Time finished:	○ ○ ○ ○ ○
Skills Practiced:	Type of Driving (Rural,City,Highway. etc):

Day Minutes:		Night Minutes:		Total Minutes:	
Carried Forward:		Carried Forward:		Carried Forward:	
Total To Date:		Total To Date:		Total To Date:	

Notes:	Instructor:
	Instructor's Signature:

Date:		Weather Conditions:

Time started:

Time finished:

☀ ⛅ 🌧 ⛈ 🌦
○ ○ ○ ○ ○

Skills Practiced:

Type of Driving (Rural,City,Highway. etc):

Day Minutes:		Night Minutes:		Total Minutes:	
Carried Forward:		Carried Forward:		Carried Forward:	
Total To Date:		Total To Date:		Total To Date:	

Notes:

Instructor:

Instructor's Signature:

Date:		Weather Conditions:

Time started:

Time finished:

☀ ⛅ 🌧 ⛈ 🌦
○ ○ ○ ○ ○

Skills Practiced:

Type of Driving (Rural,City,Highway. etc):

Day Minutes:		Night Minutes:		Total Minutes:	
Carried Forward:		Carried Forward:		Carried Forward:	
Total To Date:		Total To Date:		Total To Date:	

Notes:

Instructor:

Instructor's Signature:

Entry 1

📅 Date:	☁ Weather Conditions:	
🕐 Time started:	☀ ⛅ 🌧 ⛈ 🌨	
🕐 Time finished:	○ ○ ○ ○ ○	
💡 Skills Practiced:	📍 Type of Driving (Rural,City,Highway. etc):	

Day Minutes:		Night Minutes:		Total Minutes:	
Carried Forward:		Carried Forward:		Carried Forward:	
Total To Date:		Total To Date:		Total To Date:	

📝 Notes:	👤 Instructor:
	🖋 Instructor's Signature:

Entry 2

📅 Date:	☁ Weather Conditions:	
🕐 Time started:	☀ ⛅ 🌧 ⛈ 🌨	
🕐 Time finished:	○ ○ ○ ○ ○	
💡 Skills Practiced:	📍 Type of Driving (Rural,City,Highway. etc):	

Day Minutes:		Night Minutes:		Total Minutes:	
Carried Forward:		Carried Forward:		Carried Forward:	
Total To Date:		Total To Date:		Total To Date:	

📝 Notes:	👤 Instructor:
	🖋 Instructor's Signature:

📅 Date:		☁ Weather Conditions:
🕐 Time started:		☀ ⛅ 🌧 ⛈ 🌧
🕐 Time finished:		○ ○ ○ ○ ○
💡 Skills Practiced:		📍 Type of Driving (Rural,City,Highway. etc):

Day Minutes:		Night Minutes:		Total Minutes:	
Carried Forward:		Carried Forward:		Carried Forward:	
Total To Date:		Total To Date:		Total To Date:	

📝 Notes:	👤 Instructor:
	✒ Instructor's Signature:

📅 Date:		☁ Weather Conditions:
🕐 Time started:		☀ ⛅ 🌧 ⛈ 🌧
🕐 Time finished:		○ ○ ○ ○ ○
💡 Skills Practiced:		📍 Type of Driving (Rural,City,Highway. etc):

Day Minutes:		Night Minutes:		Total Minutes:	
Carried Forward:		Carried Forward:		Carried Forward:	
Total To Date:		Total To Date:		Total To Date:	

📝 Notes:	👤 Instructor:
	✒ Instructor's Signature:

📅 Date:	☁ Weather Conditions:

🕐 Time started:

🕐 Time finished:

☀ ⛅ 🌧 ⛈ 🌦
○ ○ ○ ○ ○

💡 Skills Practiced:

📍 Type of Driving (Rural,City,Highway. etc):

Day Minutes:		Night Minutes:		Total Minutes:	
Carried Forward:		Carried Forward:		Carried Forward:	
Total To Date:		Total To Date:		Total To Date:	

📝 Notes:

👤 Instructor:

✒ Instructor's Signature:

📅 Date:	☁ Weather Conditions:

🕐 Time started:

🕐 Time finished:

☀ ⛅ 🌧 ⛈ 🌦
○ ○ ○ ○ ○

💡 Skills Practiced:

📍 Type of Driving (Rural,City,Highway. etc):

Day Minutes:		Night Minutes:		Total Minutes:	
Carried Forward:		Carried Forward:		Carried Forward:	
Total To Date:		Total To Date:		Total To Date:	

📝 Notes:

👤 Instructor:

✒ Instructor's Signature:

Entry 1

📅 Date:		☁ Weather Conditions:

🕐 Time started:

🕐 Time finished:

☀ ⛅ 🌧 ⛈ 🌦
○ ○ ○ ○ ○

💡 Skills Practiced:

📍 Type of Driving (Rural,City,Highway. etc):

Day Minutes:		Night Minutes:		Total Minutes:	
Carried Forward:		Carried Forward:		Carried Forward:	
Total To Date:		Total To Date:		Total To Date:	

📝 Notes:

👤 Instructor:

🖊 Instructor's Signature:

Entry 2

📅 Date:		☁ Weather Conditions:

🕐 Time started:

🕐 Time finished:

☀ ⛅ 🌧 ⛈ 🌦
○ ○ ○ ○ ○

💡 Skills Practiced:

📍 Type of Driving (Rural,City,Highway. etc):

Day Minutes:		Night Minutes:		Total Minutes:	
Carried Forward:		Carried Forward:		Carried Forward:	
Total To Date:		Total To Date:		Total To Date:	

📝 Notes:

👤 Instructor:

🖊 Instructor's Signature:

📅 Date:		🌥 Weather Conditions:	

🕐 Time started:

🕐 Time finished:

Weather icons: ☀ ⛅ 🌦 ⛈ 🌧
○ ○ ○ ○ ○

💡 Skills Practiced:	📍 Type of Driving (Rural,City,Highway. etc):

Day Minutes:		Night Minutes:			Total Minutes:	
Carried Forward:		Carried Forward:			Carried Forward:	
Total To Date:		Total To Date:			Total To Date:	

📝 Notes:	👤 Instructor:
	✒ Instructor's Signature:

📅 Date:		🌥 Weather Conditions:	

🕐 Time started:

🕐 Time finished:

Weather icons: ☀ ⛅ 🌦 ⛈ 🌧
○ ○ ○ ○ ○

💡 Skills Practiced:	📍 Type of Driving (Rural,City,Highway. etc):

Day Minutes:		Night Minutes:			Total Minutes:	
Carried Forward:		Carried Forward:			Carried Forward:	
Total To Date:		Total To Date:			Total To Date:	

📝 Notes:	👤 Instructor:
	✒ Instructor's Signature:

Date:	Weather Conditions:
Time started:	☀ ⛅ 🌧 ⛈ 🌨
Time finished:	○ ○ ○ ○ ○
Skills Practiced:	Type of Driving (Rural,City,Highway. etc):

Day Minutes:		Night Minutes:		Total Minutes:	
Carried Forward:		Carried Forward:		Carried Forward:	
Total To Date:		Total To Date:		Total To Date:	

Notes:	Instructor:
	Instructor's Signature:

Date:	Weather Conditions:
Time started:	☀ ⛅ 🌧 ⛈ 🌨
Time finished:	○ ○ ○ ○ ○
Skills Practiced:	Type of Driving (Rural,City,Highway. etc):

Day Minutes:		Night Minutes:		Total Minutes:	
Carried Forward:		Carried Forward:		Carried Forward:	
Total To Date:		Total To Date:		Total To Date:	

Notes:	Instructor:
	Instructor's Signature:

Entry 1

Date:		Weather Conditions:
Time started:		☀ ⛅ 🌧 ⛈ 🌨
Time finished:		○ ○ ○ ○ ○
Skills Practiced:		Type of Driving (Rural,City,Highway. etc):

Day Minutes:		Night Minutes:			Total Minutes:	
Carried Forward:		Carried Forward:			Carried Forward:	
Total To Date:		Total To Date:			Total To Date:	

Notes:	Instructor:
	Instructor's Signature:

Entry 2

Date:		Weather Conditions:
Time started:		☀ ⛅ 🌧 ⛈ 🌨
Time finished:		○ ○ ○ ○ ○
Skills Practiced:		Type of Driving (Rural,City,Highway. etc):

Day Minutes:		Night Minutes:			Total Minutes:	
Carried Forward:		Carried Forward:			Carried Forward:	
Total To Date:		Total To Date:			Total To Date:	

Notes:	Instructor:
	Instructor's Signature:

Entry 1

📅 Date:		☁ Weather Conditions:
🕐 Time started:		☀ ⛅ 🌧 ⛈ 🌧
🕐 Time finished:		○ ○ ○ ○ ○
💡 Skills Practiced:		📍 Type of Driving (Rural,City,Highway. etc):

Day Minutes:		Night Minutes:		Total Minutes:	
Carried Forward:		Carried Forward:		Carried Forward:	
Total To Date:		Total To Date:		Total To Date:	

📝 Notes:	🧑 Instructor:
	✒ Instructor's Signature:

Entry 2

📅 Date:		☁ Weather Conditions:
🕐 Time started:		☀ ⛅ 🌧 ⛈ 🌧
🕐 Time finished:		○ ○ ○ ○ ○
💡 Skills Practiced:		📍 Type of Driving (Rural,City,Highway. etc):

Day Minutes:		Night Minutes:		Total Minutes:	
Carried Forward:		Carried Forward:		Carried Forward:	
Total To Date:		Total To Date:		Total To Date:	

📝 Notes:	🧑 Instructor:
	✒ Instructor's Signature:

Entry 1

Date:		Weather Conditions:
Time started:		☀ ⛅ 🌧 ⛈ 🌦
Time finished:		○ ○ ○ ○ ○
Skills Practiced:		Type of Driving (Rural,City,Highway. etc):

Day Minutes:		Night Minutes:			Total Minutes:	
Carried Forward:		Carried Forward:			Carried Forward:	
Total To Date:		Total To Date:			Total To Date:	

Notes:	Instructor:
	Instructor's Signature:

Entry 2

Date:		Weather Conditions:
Time started:		☀ ⛅ 🌧 ⛈ 🌦
Time finished:		○ ○ ○ ○ ○
Skills Practiced:		Type of Driving (Rural,City,Highway. etc):

Day Minutes:		Night Minutes:			Total Minutes:	
Carried Forward:		Carried Forward:			Carried Forward:	
Total To Date:		Total To Date:			Total To Date:	

Notes:	Instructor:
	Instructor's Signature:

Entry 1

Date:		Weather Conditions:			
Time started:		☀ ⛅ 🌦 ⛈ 🌨			
Time finished:		○ ○ ○ ○ ○			
Skills Practiced:		Type of Driving (Rural,City,Highway. etc):			

Day Minutes:		Night Minutes:		Total Minutes:	
Carried Forward:		Carried Forward:		Carried Forward:	
Total To Date:		Total To Date:		Total To Date:	

Notes:	Instructor:
	Instructor's Signature:

Entry 2

Date:		Weather Conditions:			
Time started:		☀ ⛅ 🌦 ⛈ 🌨			
Time finished:		○ ○ ○ ○ ○			
Skills Practiced:		Type of Driving (Rural,City,Highway. etc):			

Day Minutes:		Night Minutes:		Total Minutes:	
Carried Forward:		Carried Forward:		Carried Forward:	
Total To Date:		Total To Date:		Total To Date:	

Notes:	Instructor:
	Instructor's Signature:

Date:	Weather Conditions:

Time started:

Time finished:

Skills Practiced:

Type of Driving (Rural,City,Highway. etc):

Day Minutes:		Night Minutes:			Total Minutes:	
Carried Forward:		Carried Forward:			Carried Forward:	
Total To Date:		Total To Date:			Total To Date:	

Notes:

Instructor:

Instructor's Signature:

Date:	Weather Conditions:

Time started:

Time finished:

Skills Practiced:

Type of Driving (Rural,City,Highway. etc):

Day Minutes:		Night Minutes:			Total Minutes:	
Carried Forward:		Carried Forward:			Carried Forward:	
Total To Date:		Total To Date:			Total To Date:	

Notes:

Instructor:

Instructor's Signature:

Entry 1

Date:		Weather Conditions:

Time started:

Time finished:

☀ 　 ⛅ 　 🌧 　 ⛈ 　 🌨
○ 　 ○ 　 ○ 　 ○ 　 ○

Skills Practiced:

Type of Driving (Rural,City,Highway. etc):

Day Minutes:		Night Minutes:		Total Minutes:	
Carried Forward:		Carried Forward:		Carried Forward:	
Total To Date:		Total To Date:		Total To Date:	

Notes:

Instructor:

Instructor's Signature:

Entry 2

Date:		Weather Conditions:

Time started:

Time finished:

☀ 　 ⛅ 　 🌧 　 ⛈ 　 🌨
○ 　 ○ 　 ○ 　 ○ 　 ○

Skills Practiced:

Type of Driving (Rural,City,Highway. etc):

Day Minutes:		Night Minutes:		Total Minutes:	
Carried Forward:		Carried Forward:		Carried Forward:	
Total To Date:		Total To Date:		Total To Date:	

Notes:

Instructor:

Instructor's Signature:

📅 Date:	☁ Weather Conditions:

🕐 Time started:

🕐 Time finished:

☀ 🌤 🌧 ⛈ 🌨
○ ○ ○ ○ ○

💡 Skills Practiced:

📍 Type of Driving (Rural,City,Highway. etc):

Day Minutes:		Night Minutes:		Total Minutes:	
Carried Forward:		Carried Forward:		Carried Forward:	
Total To Date:		Total To Date:		Total To Date:	

📝 Notes:

👤 Instructor:

🖊 Instructor's Signature:

📅 Date:	☁ Weather Conditions:

🕐 Time started:

🕐 Time finished:

☀ 🌤 🌧 ⛈ 🌨
○ ○ ○ ○ ○

💡 Skills Practiced:

📍 Type of Driving (Rural,City,Highway. etc):

Day Minutes:		Night Minutes:		Total Minutes:	
Carried Forward:		Carried Forward:		Carried Forward:	
Total To Date:		Total To Date:		Total To Date:	

📝 Notes:

👤 Instructor:

🖊 Instructor's Signature:

📅 Date:	☁ Weather Conditions:

🕐 Time started:	☀ ⛅ 🌧 ⛈ 🌨
🕐 Time finished:	○ ○ ○ ○ ○

💡 Skills Practiced:	📍 Type of Driving (Rural,City,Highway. etc):

Day Minutes:		Night Minutes:		Total Minutes:	
Carried Forward:		Carried Forward:		Carried Forward:	
Total To Date:		Total To Date:		Total To Date:	

📝 Notes:	👤 Instructor:
	✍ Instructor's Signature:

📅 Date:	☁ Weather Conditions:

🕐 Time started:	☀ ⛅ 🌧 ⛈ 🌨
🕐 Time finished:	○ ○ ○ ○ ○

💡 Skills Practiced:	📍 Type of Driving (Rural,City,Highway. etc):

Day Minutes:		Night Minutes:		Total Minutes:	
Carried Forward:		Carried Forward:		Carried Forward:	
Total To Date:		Total To Date:		Total To Date:	

📝 Notes:	👤 Instructor:
	✍ Instructor's Signature:

Entry 1

📅 Date:	☁ Weather Conditions:
🕐 Time started:	☀ ⛅ 🌧 ⛈ 🌨
🕐 Time finished:	○ ○ ○ ○ ○
💡 Skills Practiced:	📍 Type of Driving (Rural,City,Highway. etc):

Day Minutes:		Night Minutes:		Total Minutes:	
Carried Forward:		Carried Forward:		Carried Forward:	
Total To Date:		Total To Date:		Total To Date:	

📝 Notes:	👤 Instructor:
	🖊 Instructor's Signature:

Entry 2

📅 Date:	☁ Weather Conditions:
🕐 Time started:	☀ ⛅ 🌧 ⛈ 🌨
🕐 Time finished:	○ ○ ○ ○ ○
💡 Skills Practiced:	📍 Type of Driving (Rural,City,Highway. etc):

Day Minutes:		Night Minutes:		Total Minutes:	
Carried Forward:		Carried Forward:		Carried Forward:	
Total To Date:		Total To Date:		Total To Date:	

📝 Notes:	👤 Instructor:
	🖊 Instructor's Signature:

📅 Date:	☁ Weather Conditions:

🕐 Time started:	☀ ⛅ 🌧 ⛈ 🌧
🕐 Time finished:	○ ○ ○ ○ ○

💡 Skills Practiced:	📍 Type of Driving (Rural,City,Highway. etc):

Day Minutes:		Night Minutes:		Total Minutes:	
Carried Forward:		Carried Forward:		Carried Forward:	
Total To Date:		Total To Date:		Total To Date:	

📝 Notes:	👤 Instructor:
	✒ Instructor's Signature:

📅 Date:	☁ Weather Conditions:

🕐 Time started:	☀ ⛅ 🌧 ⛈ 🌧
🕐 Time finished:	○ ○ ○ ○ ○

💡 Skills Practiced:	📍 Type of Driving (Rural,City,Highway. etc):

Day Minutes:		Night Minutes:		Total Minutes:	
Carried Forward:		Carried Forward:		Carried Forward:	
Total To Date:		Total To Date:		Total To Date:	

📝 Notes:	👤 Instructor:
	✒ Instructor's Signature:

Date:	Weather Conditions:
Time started:	☀ ⛅ 🌧 ⛈ 🌧
Time finished:	○ ○ ○ ○ ○
Skills Practiced:	Type of Driving (Rural,City,Highway. etc):

Day Minutes:		Night Minutes:			Total Minutes:	
Carried Forward:		Carried Forward:			Carried Forward:	
Total To Date:		Total To Date:			Total To Date:	

Notes:	Instructor:
	Instructor's Signature:

Date:	Weather Conditions:
Time started:	☀ ⛅ 🌧 ⛈ 🌧
Time finished:	○ ○ ○ ○ ○
Skills Practiced:	Type of Driving (Rural,City,Highway. etc):

Day Minutes:		Night Minutes:			Total Minutes:	
Carried Forward:		Carried Forward:			Carried Forward:	
Total To Date:		Total To Date:			Total To Date:	

Notes:	Instructor:
	Instructor's Signature:

Date:			Weather Conditions:		

Time started:		
Time finished:		

☀ ○   ⛅ ○   🌦 ○   ⛈ ○   🌧 ○

Skills Practiced:			Type of Driving (Rural, City, Highway. etc):		

Day Minutes:		Night Minutes:		Total Minutes:	
Carried Forward:		Carried Forward:		Carried Forward:	
Total To Date:		Total To Date:		Total To Date:	

Notes:	Instructor:
	Instructor's Signature:

Date:			Weather Conditions:		

Time started:		
Time finished:		

☀ ○   ⛅ ○   🌦 ○   ⛈ ○   🌧 ○

Skills Practiced:			Type of Driving (Rural, City, Highway. etc):		

Day Minutes:		Night Minutes:		Total Minutes:	
Carried Forward:		Carried Forward:		Carried Forward:	
Total To Date:		Total To Date:		Total To Date:	

Notes:	Instructor:
	Instructor's Signature:

Entry 1

Date:	Weather Conditions:
Time started:	☀ ⛅ 🌧 ⛈ 🌨
Time finished:	○ ○ ○ ○ ○
Skills Practiced:	Type of Driving (Rural,City,Highway. etc):

Day Minutes:		Night Minutes:		Total Minutes:	
Carried Forward:		Carried Forward:		Carried Forward:	
Total To Date:		Total To Date:		Total To Date:	

Notes:	Instructor:
	Instructor's Signature:

Entry 2

Date:	Weather Conditions:
Time started:	☀ ⛅ 🌧 ⛈ 🌨
Time finished:	○ ○ ○ ○ ○
Skills Practiced:	Type of Driving (Rural,City,Highway. etc):

Day Minutes:		Night Minutes:		Total Minutes:	
Carried Forward:		Carried Forward:		Carried Forward:	
Total To Date:		Total To Date:		Total To Date:	

Notes:	Instructor:
	Instructor's Signature:

Date:	Weather Conditions:

Time started:	
Time finished:	☀ ⛅ 🌧 ⛈ 🌨
	○ ○ ○ ○ ○

Skills Practiced:	Type of Driving (Rural,City,Highway. etc):

Day Minutes:		Night Minutes:		Total Minutes:	
Carried Forward:		Carried Forward:		Carried Forward:	
Total To Date:		Total To Date:		Total To Date:	

Notes:	Instructor:
	Instructor's Signature:

Date:	Weather Conditions:

Time started:	
Time finished:	☀ ⛅ 🌧 ⛈ 🌨
	○ ○ ○ ○ ○

Skills Practiced:	Type of Driving (Rural,City,Highway. etc):

Day Minutes:		Night Minutes:		Total Minutes:	
Carried Forward:		Carried Forward:		Carried Forward:	
Total To Date:		Total To Date:		Total To Date:	

Notes:	Instructor:
	Instructor's Signature:

Date:		Weather Conditions:

Time started:		☀ ⛅ 🌧 ⛈ 🌨
Time finished:		○ ○ ○ ○ ○

Skills Practiced:		Type of Driving (Rural,City,Highway. etc):

Day Minutes:		Night Minutes:			Total Minutes:	
Carried Forward:		Carried Forward:			Carried Forward:	
Total To Date:		Total To Date:			Total To Date:	

Notes:		Instructor:
		Instructor's Signature:

Date:		Weather Conditions:

Time started:		☀ ⛅ 🌧 ⛈ 🌨
Time finished:		○ ○ ○ ○ ○

Skills Practiced:		Type of Driving (Rural,City,Highway. etc):

Day Minutes:		Night Minutes:			Total Minutes:	
Carried Forward:		Carried Forward:			Carried Forward:	
Total To Date:		Total To Date:			Total To Date:	

Notes:		Instructor:
		Instructor's Signature:

Entry 1

📅 Date:			
🕐 Time started:			
🕐 Time finished:			

☁ Weather Conditions:

☀ ○   ⛅ ○   🌧 ○   ⛈ ○   🌨 ○

💡 Skills Practiced:

📍 Type of Driving (Rural,City,Highway. etc):

Day Minutes:		Night Minutes:		Total Minutes:	
Carried Forward:		Carried Forward:		Carried Forward:	
Total To Date:		Total To Date:		Total To Date:	

📝 Notes:

👤 Instructor:

✍ Instructor's Signature:

Entry 2

📅 Date:			
🕐 Time started:			
🕐 Time finished:			

☁ Weather Conditions:

☀ ○   ⛅ ○   🌧 ○   ⛈ ○   🌨 ○

💡 Skills Practiced:

📍 Type of Driving (Rural,City,Highway. etc):

Day Minutes:		Night Minutes:		Total Minutes:	
Carried Forward:		Carried Forward:		Carried Forward:	
Total To Date:		Total To Date:		Total To Date:	

📝 Notes:

👤 Instructor:

✍ Instructor's Signature:

Date:	Weather Conditions:
Time started:	☀ ⛅ 🌧 ⛈ 🌨
Time finished:	○ ○ ○ ○ ○
Skills Practiced:	Type of Driving (Rural,City,Highway. etc):

Day Minutes:		Night Minutes:			Total Minutes:	
Carried Forward:		Carried Forward:			Carried Forward:	
Total To Date:		Total To Date:			Total To Date:	

Notes:	Instructor:
	Instructor's Signature:

Date:	Weather Conditions:
Time started:	☀ ⛅ 🌧 ⛈ 🌨
Time finished:	○ ○ ○ ○ ○
Skills Practiced:	Type of Driving (Rural,City,Highway. etc):

Day Minutes:		Night Minutes:			Total Minutes:	
Carried Forward:		Carried Forward:			Carried Forward:	
Total To Date:		Total To Date:			Total To Date:	

Notes:	Instructor:
	Instructor's Signature:

Entry 1

📅 Date:		
🕐 Time started:		
🕐 Time finished:		

☁ Weather Conditions:

☀ ⛅ 🌧 ⛈ 🌨
○ ○ ○ ○ ○

💡 Skills Practiced:

📍 Type of Driving (Rural,City,Highway. etc):

Day Minutes:		Night Minutes:		Total Minutes:	
Carried Forward:		Carried Forward:		Carried Forward:	
Total To Date:		Total To Date:		Total To Date:	

📝 Notes:

👤 Instructor:

🖊 Instructor's Signature:

Entry 2

📅 Date:		
🕐 Time started:		
🕐 Time finished:		

☁ Weather Conditions:

☀ ⛅ 🌧 ⛈ 🌨
○ ○ ○ ○ ○

💡 Skills Practiced:

📍 Type of Driving (Rural,City,Highway. etc):

Day Minutes:		Night Minutes:		Total Minutes:	
Carried Forward:		Carried Forward:		Carried Forward:	
Total To Date:		Total To Date:		Total To Date:	

📝 Notes:

👤 Instructor:

🖊 Instructor's Signature:

Entry 1

📅 Date: _____

🕐 Time started: _____

🕐 Time finished: _____

💡 Skills Practiced:

☁ Weather Conditions:

☀ ⛅ 🌧 ⛈ 🌦
○ ○ ○ ○ ○

📍 Type of Driving (Rural,City,Highway. etc):

Day Minutes:		Night Minutes:		Total Minutes:	
Carried Forward:		Carried Forward:		Carried Forward:	
Total To Date:		Total To Date:		Total To Date:	

📝 Notes:

👤 Instructor:

✍ Instructor's Signature:

Entry 2

📅 Date: _____

🕐 Time started: _____

🕐 Time finished: _____

💡 Skills Practiced:

☁ Weather Conditions:

☀ ⛅ 🌧 ⛈ 🌦
○ ○ ○ ○ ○

📍 Type of Driving (Rural,City,Highway. etc):

Day Minutes:		Night Minutes:		Total Minutes:	
Carried Forward:		Carried Forward:		Carried Forward:	
Total To Date:		Total To Date:		Total To Date:	

📝 Notes:

👤 Instructor:

✍ Instructor's Signature:

Date:

Time started:

Time finished:

Weather Conditions:

Skills Practiced:

Type of Driving (Rural,City,Highway. etc):

Day Minutes:		Night Minutes:			Total Minutes:	
Carried Forward:		Carried Forward:			Carried Forward:	
Total To Date:		Total To Date:			Total To Date:	

Notes:

Instructor:

Instructor's Signature:

Date:

Time started:

Time finished:

Weather Conditions:

Skills Practiced:

Type of Driving (Rural,City,Highway. etc):

Day Minutes:		Night Minutes:			Total Minutes:	
Carried Forward:		Carried Forward:			Carried Forward:	
Total To Date:		Total To Date:			Total To Date:	

Notes:

Instructor:

Instructor's Signature:

Entry 1

Date:		Weather Conditions:

Time started:

Time finished:

Weather options: ☀ ⛅ 🌧 ⛈ 🌧 (○ ○ ○ ○ ○)

Skills Practiced:

Type of Driving (Rural, City, Highway. etc):

Day Minutes:		Night Minutes:		Total Minutes:	
Carried Forward:		Carried Forward:		Carried Forward:	
Total To Date:		Total To Date:		Total To Date:	

Notes:

Instructor:

Instructor's Signature:

Entry 2

Date:		Weather Conditions:

Time started:

Time finished:

Weather options: ☀ ⛅ 🌧 ⛈ 🌧 (○ ○ ○ ○ ○)

Skills Practiced:

Type of Driving (Rural, City, Highway. etc):

Day Minutes:		Night Minutes:		Total Minutes:	
Carried Forward:		Carried Forward:		Carried Forward:	
Total To Date:		Total To Date:		Total To Date:	

Notes:

Instructor:

Instructor's Signature:

📅 Date:	☁ Weather Conditions:

🕐 Time started:	
🕐 Time finished:	☀ ⛅ 🌧 ⛈ 🌨
	○ ○ ○ ○ ○

💡 Skills Practiced:	📍 Type of Driving (Rural,City,Highway. etc):

Day Minutes:		Night Minutes:		Total Minutes:	
Carried Forward:		Carried Forward:		Carried Forward:	
Total To Date:		Total To Date:		Total To Date:	

📝 Notes:	👤 Instructor:
	✍ Instructor's Signature:

📅 Date:	☁ Weather Conditions:

🕐 Time started:	
🕐 Time finished:	☀ ⛅ 🌧 ⛈ 🌨
	○ ○ ○ ○ ○

💡 Skills Practiced:	📍 Type of Driving (Rural,City,Highway. etc):

Day Minutes:		Night Minutes:		Total Minutes:	
Carried Forward:		Carried Forward:		Carried Forward:	
Total To Date:		Total To Date:		Total To Date:	

📝 Notes:	👤 Instructor:
	✍ Instructor's Signature:

Entry 1

	Date:
	Time started:
	Time finished:
	Skills Practiced:

Weather Conditions:

○ ○ ○ ○ ○

Type of Driving (Rural, City, Highway. etc):

Day Minutes:		Night Minutes:			Total Minutes:	
Carried Forward:		Carried Forward:			Carried Forward:	
Total To Date:		Total To Date:			Total To Date:	

Notes:	Instructor:
	Instructor's Signature:

Entry 2

	Date:
	Time started:
	Time finished:
	Skills Practiced:

Weather Conditions:

○ ○ ○ ○ ○

Type of Driving (Rural, City, Highway. etc):

Day Minutes:		Night Minutes:			Total Minutes:	
Carried Forward:		Carried Forward:			Carried Forward:	
Total To Date:		Total To Date:			Total To Date:	

Notes:	Instructor:
	Instructor's Signature:

📅 Date:	☁ Weather Conditions:

🕐 Time started:	☀ ⛅ 🌧 ⛈ 🌨
🕐 Time finished:	○ ○ ○ ○ ○

💡 Skills Practiced:	📍 Type of Driving (Rural,City,Highway. etc):

Day Minutes:		Night Minutes:		Total Minutes:	
Carried Forward:		Carried Forward:		Carried Forward:	
Total To Date:		Total To Date:		Total To Date:	

📝 Notes:	👤 Instructor:
	✒ Instructor's Signature:

📅 Date:	☁ Weather Conditions:

🕐 Time started:	☀ ⛅ 🌧 ⛈ 🌨
🕐 Time finished:	○ ○ ○ ○ ○

💡 Skills Practiced:	📍 Type of Driving (Rural,City,Highway. etc):

Day Minutes:		Night Minutes:		Total Minutes:	
Carried Forward:		Carried Forward:		Carried Forward:	
Total To Date:		Total To Date:		Total To Date:	

📝 Notes:	👤 Instructor:
	✒ Instructor's Signature:

📅 Date:	☁ Weather Conditions:
🕐 Time started:	☀ ⛅ 🌧 ⛈ 🌨
🕐 Time finished:	○ ○ ○ ○ ○
💡 Skills Practiced:	📍 Type of Driving (Rural,City,Highway. etc):

Day Minutes:		Night Minutes:			Total Minutes:	
Carried Forward:		Carried Forward:			Carried Forward:	
Total To Date:		Total To Date:			Total To Date:	

📝 Notes:	👤 Instructor:
	✍ Instructor's Signature:

📅 Date:	☁ Weather Conditions:
🕐 Time started:	☀ ⛅ 🌧 ⛈ 🌨
🕐 Time finished:	○ ○ ○ ○ ○
💡 Skills Practiced:	📍 Type of Driving (Rural,City,Highway. etc):

Day Minutes:		Night Minutes:			Total Minutes:	
Carried Forward:		Carried Forward:			Carried Forward:	
Total To Date:		Total To Date:			Total To Date:	

📝 Notes:	👤 Instructor:
	✍ Instructor's Signature:

Entry 1

Date:		Weather Conditions:

Time started:

Time finished:

Skills Practiced:

Type of Driving (Rural, City, Highway. etc):

Day Minutes:		Night Minutes:		Total Minutes:	
Carried Forward:		Carried Forward:		Carried Forward:	
Total To Date:		Total To Date:		Total To Date:	

Notes:

Instructor:

Instructor's Signature:

Entry 2

Date:		Weather Conditions:

Time started:

Time finished:

Skills Practiced:

Type of Driving (Rural, City, Highway. etc):

Day Minutes:		Night Minutes:		Total Minutes:	
Carried Forward:		Carried Forward:		Carried Forward:	
Total To Date:		Total To Date:		Total To Date:	

Notes:

Instructor:

Instructor's Signature:

Entry 1

Date:			Weather Conditions: ☀ ⛅ 🌧 ⛈ 🌨 ○ ○ ○ ○ ○
Time started:			
Time finished:			
Skills Practiced:			Type of Driving (Rural,City,Highway. etc):

Day Minutes:		Night Minutes:			Total Minutes:	
Carried Forward:		Carried Forward:			Carried Forward:	
Total To Date:		Total To Date:			Total To Date:	

Notes:

Instructor:

Instructor's Signature:

Entry 2

Date:			Weather Conditions: ☀ ⛅ 🌧 ⛈ 🌨 ○ ○ ○ ○ ○
Time started:			
Time finished:			
Skills Practiced:			Type of Driving (Rural,City,Highway. etc):

Day Minutes:		Night Minutes:			Total Minutes:	
Carried Forward:		Carried Forward:			Carried Forward:	
Total To Date:		Total To Date:			Total To Date:	

Notes:

Instructor:

Instructor's Signature:

Date:		Weather Conditions:

Time started:

Time finished:

☀ 🌤 🌧 ⛈ 🌨
○ ○ ○ ○ ○

Skills Practiced:

Type of Driving (Rural, City, Highway. etc):

Day Minutes:		Night Minutes:		Total Minutes:	
Carried Forward:		Carried Forward:		Carried Forward:	
Total To Date:		Total To Date:		Total To Date:	

Notes:

Instructor:

Instructor's Signature:

Date:		Weather Conditions:

Time started:

Time finished:

☀ 🌤 🌧 ⛈ 🌨
○ ○ ○ ○ ○

Skills Practiced:

Type of Driving (Rural, City, Highway. etc):

Day Minutes:		Night Minutes:		Total Minutes:	
Carried Forward:		Carried Forward:		Carried Forward:	
Total To Date:		Total To Date:		Total To Date:	

Notes:

Instructor:

Instructor's Signature:

Entry 1

📅 Date:		🌥 Weather Conditions:				
🕐 Time started:		☀ ⛅ 🌧 ⛈ 🌨				
🕐 Time finished:		○ ○ ○ ○ ○				
💡 Skills Practiced:		📍 Type of Driving (Rural,City,Highway. etc):				

Day Minutes:		Night Minutes:			Total Minutes:	
Carried Forward:		Carried Forward:			Carried Forward:	
Total To Date:		Total To Date:			Total To Date:	

📝 Notes:	👤 Instructor:
	✒ Instructor's Signature:

Entry 2

📅 Date:		🌥 Weather Conditions:				
🕐 Time started:		☀ ⛅ 🌧 ⛈ 🌨				
🕐 Time finished:		○ ○ ○ ○ ○				
💡 Skills Practiced:		📍 Type of Driving (Rural,City,Highway. etc):				

Day Minutes:		Night Minutes:			Total Minutes:	
Carried Forward:		Carried Forward:			Carried Forward:	
Total To Date:		Total To Date:			Total To Date:	

📝 Notes:	👤 Instructor:
	✒ Instructor's Signature:

📅 Date:			☁ Weather Conditions:		
🕐 Time started:					
🕐 Time finished:			☀ ⛅ 🌧 ⛈ 🌧 ○ ○ ○ ○ ○		
💡 Skills Practiced:			📍 Type of Driving (Rural,City,Highway. etc):		

Day Minutes:		Night Minutes:		Total Minutes:	
Carried Forward:		Carried Forward:		Carried Forward:	
Total To Date:		Total To Date:		Total To Date:	

📝 Notes:	👤 Instructor:
	🖋 Instructor's Signature:

📅 Date:			☁ Weather Conditions:		
🕐 Time started:					
🕐 Time finished:			☀ ⛅ 🌧 ⛈ 🌧 ○ ○ ○ ○ ○		
💡 Skills Practiced:			📍 Type of Driving (Rural,City,Highway. etc):		

Day Minutes:		Night Minutes:		Total Minutes:	
Carried Forward:		Carried Forward:		Carried Forward:	
Total To Date:		Total To Date:		Total To Date:	

📝 Notes:	👤 Instructor:
	🖋 Instructor's Signature:

Date:	Weather Conditions:
Time started:	☀ ⛅ 🌧 ⛈ 🌨
Time finished:	○ ○ ○ ○ ○
Skills Practiced:	Type of Driving (Rural,City,Highway. etc):

Day Minutes:		Night Minutes:			Total Minutes:	
Carried Forward:		Carried Forward:			Carried Forward:	
Total To Date:		Total To Date:			Total To Date:	

Notes:	Instructor:
	Instructor's Signature:

Date:	Weather Conditions:
Time started:	☀ ⛅ 🌧 ⛈ 🌨
Time finished:	○ ○ ○ ○ ○
Skills Practiced:	Type of Driving (Rural,City,Highway. etc):

Day Minutes:		Night Minutes:			Total Minutes:	
Carried Forward:		Carried Forward:			Carried Forward:	
Total To Date:		Total To Date:			Total To Date:	

Notes:	Instructor:
	Instructor's Signature:

📅 Date:			☁ Weather Conditions:	

🕐 Time started:		☀ 🌤 🌧 ⛈ 🌦
🕐 Time finished:		○ ○ ○ ○ ○

💡 Skills Practiced:	📍 Type of Driving (Rural, City, Highway. etc):

Day Minutes:		Night Minutes:			Total Minutes:	
Carried Forward:		Carried Forward:			Carried Forward:	
Total To Date:		Total To Date:			Total To Date:	

📝 Notes:	👤 Instructor:
	✒ Instructor's Signature:

📅 Date:			☁ Weather Conditions:	

🕐 Time started:		☀ 🌤 🌧 ⛈ 🌦
🕐 Time finished:		○ ○ ○ ○ ○

💡 Skills Practiced:	📍 Type of Driving (Rural, City, Highway. etc):

Day Minutes:		Night Minutes:			Total Minutes:	
Carried Forward:		Carried Forward:			Carried Forward:	
Total To Date:		Total To Date:			Total To Date:	

📝 Notes:	👤 Instructor:
	✒ Instructor's Signature:

📅 Date:	🌥 Weather Conditions:

Time started: _____

Time finished: _____

☀ ⛅ 🌧 ⛈ 🌨
○ ○ ○ ○ ○

💡 Skills Practiced:	📍 Type of Driving (Rural,City,Highway. etc):

Day Minutes:		Night Minutes:			Total Minutes:	
Carried Forward:		Carried Forward:			Carried Forward:	
Total To Date:		Total To Date:			Total To Date:	

📝 Notes:	👤 Instructor:
	✍ Instructor's Signature:

📅 Date:	🌥 Weather Conditions:

Time started: _____

Time finished: _____

☀ ⛅ 🌧 ⛈ 🌨
○ ○ ○ ○ ○

💡 Skills Practiced:	📍 Type of Driving (Rural,City,Highway. etc):

Day Minutes:		Night Minutes:			Total Minutes:	
Carried Forward:		Carried Forward:			Carried Forward:	
Total To Date:		Total To Date:			Total To Date:	

📝 Notes:	👤 Instructor:
	✍ Instructor's Signature:

📅 Date:		🌥 Weather Conditions:		
🕐 Time started:		☀ ⛅ 🌧 ⛈ 🌨		
🕐 Time finished:		○ ○ ○ ○ ○		
💡 Skills Practiced:		📍 Type of Driving (Rural,City,Highway. etc):		

Day Minutes:		Night Minutes:		Total Minutes:	
Carried Forward:		Carried Forward:		Carried Forward:	
Total To Date:		Total To Date:		Total To Date:	

📝 Notes:	👤 Instructor:
	✍ Instructor's Signature:

📅 Date:		🌥 Weather Conditions:		
🕐 Time started:		☀ ⛅ 🌧 ⛈ 🌨		
🕐 Time finished:		○ ○ ○ ○ ○		
💡 Skills Practiced:		📍 Type of Driving (Rural,City,Highway. etc):		

Day Minutes:		Night Minutes:		Total Minutes:	
Carried Forward:		Carried Forward:		Carried Forward:	
Total To Date:		Total To Date:		Total To Date:	

📝 Notes:	👤 Instructor:
	✍ Instructor's Signature:

Entry 1

| Date: | Weather Conditions: |

Time started:

Time finished:

Skills Practiced:

Type of Driving (Rural, City, Highway. etc):

Day Minutes:		Night Minutes:		Total Minutes:	
Carried Forward:		Carried Forward:		Carried Forward:	
Total To Date:		Total To Date:		Total To Date:	

Notes:

Instructor:

Instructor's Signature:

Entry 2

| Date: | Weather Conditions: |

Time started:

Time finished:

Skills Practiced:

Type of Driving (Rural, City, Highway. etc):

Day Minutes:		Night Minutes:		Total Minutes:	
Carried Forward:		Carried Forward:		Carried Forward:	
Total To Date:		Total To Date:		Total To Date:	

Notes:

Instructor:

Instructor's Signature:

📅 Date:	☁ Weather Conditions:

🕐 Time started:	☀ ⛅ 🌧 ⛈ 🌨
🕐 Time finished:	○ ○ ○ ○ ○

💡 Skills Practiced:	📍 Type of Driving (Rural,City,Highway. etc):

Day Minutes:		Night Minutes:			Total Minutes:	
Carried Forward:		Carried Forward:			Carried Forward:	
Total To Date:		Total To Date:			Total To Date:	

📝 Notes:	👤 Instructor:
	✍ Instructor's Signature:

📅 Date:	☁ Weather Conditions:

🕐 Time started:	☀ ⛅ 🌧 ⛈ 🌨
🕐 Time finished:	○ ○ ○ ○ ○

💡 Skills Practiced:	📍 Type of Driving (Rural,City,Highway. etc):

Day Minutes:		Night Minutes:			Total Minutes:	
Carried Forward:		Carried Forward:			Carried Forward:	
Total To Date:		Total To Date:			Total To Date:	

📝 Notes:	👤 Instructor:
	✍ Instructor's Signature:

Entry 1

📅 Date: _____

🕐 Time started: _____

🕐 Time finished: _____

☁ Weather Conditions:

☀ ○   ⛅ ○   🌧 ○   ⛈ ○   🌦 ○

💡 Skills Practiced:

📍 Type of Driving (Rural, City, Highway. etc):

Day Minutes:		Night Minutes:		Total Minutes:	
Carried Forward:		Carried Forward:		Carried Forward:	
Total To Date:		Total To Date:		Total To Date:	

📝 Notes:

👤 Instructor:

🖋 Instructor's Signature:

Entry 2

📅 Date: _____

🕐 Time started: _____

🕐 Time finished: _____

☁ Weather Conditions:

☀ ○   ⛅ ○   🌧 ○   ⛈ ○   🌦 ○

💡 Skills Practiced:

📍 Type of Driving (Rural, City, Highway. etc):

Day Minutes:		Night Minutes:		Total Minutes:	
Carried Forward:		Carried Forward:		Carried Forward:	
Total To Date:		Total To Date:		Total To Date:	

📝 Notes:

👤 Instructor:

🖋 Instructor's Signature:

Date:		Weather Conditions:

☼ ◯   ☁ ◯   🌧 ◯   ⛈ ◯   🌧 ◯

Time started:	
Time finished:	

Skills Practiced:

Type of Driving (Rural, City, Highway. etc):

Day Minutes:		Night Minutes:		Total Minutes:	
Carried Forward:		Carried Forward:		Carried Forward:	
Total To Date:		Total To Date:		Total To Date:	

Notes:

Instructor:

Instructor's Signature:

Date:		Weather Conditions:

☼ ◯   ☁ ◯   🌧 ◯   ⛈ ◯   🌧 ◯

Time started:	
Time finished:	

Skills Practiced:

Type of Driving (Rural, City, Highway. etc):

Day Minutes:		Night Minutes:		Total Minutes:	
Carried Forward:		Carried Forward:		Carried Forward:	
Total To Date:		Total To Date:		Total To Date:	

Notes:

Instructor:

Instructor's Signature:

Entry 1

Date:		Weather Conditions:

☀ ⛅ 🌧 ⛈ 🌦
○ ○ ○ ○ ○

Time started:	
Time finished:	

Skills Practiced:

Type of Driving (Rural,City,Highway. etc):

Day Minutes:		Night Minutes:		Total Minutes:	
Carried Forward:		Carried Forward:		Carried Forward:	
Total To Date:		Total To Date:		Total To Date:	

Notes:

Instructor:

Instructor's Signature:

Entry 2

Date:		Weather Conditions:

☀ ⛅ 🌧 ⛈ 🌦
○ ○ ○ ○ ○

Time started:	
Time finished:	

Skills Practiced:

Type of Driving (Rural,City,Highway. etc):

Day Minutes:		Night Minutes:		Total Minutes:	
Carried Forward:		Carried Forward:		Carried Forward:	
Total To Date:		Total To Date:		Total To Date:	

Notes:

Instructor:

Instructor's Signature:

Date:		Weather Conditions:

Time started:

Time finished:

☀ ⛅ 🌧 ⛈ 🌧
○ ○ ○ ○ ○

Skills Practiced:

Type of Driving (Rural, City, Highway. etc):

Day Minutes:		Night Minutes:		Total Minutes:	
Carried Forward:		Carried Forward:		Carried Forward:	
Total To Date:		Total To Date:		Total To Date:	

Notes:

Instructor:

Instructor's Signature:

Date:		Weather Conditions:

Time started:

Time finished:

☀ ⛅ 🌧 ⛈ 🌧
○ ○ ○ ○ ○

Skills Practiced:

Type of Driving (Rural, City, Highway. etc):

Day Minutes:		Night Minutes:		Total Minutes:	
Carried Forward:		Carried Forward:		Carried Forward:	
Total To Date:		Total To Date:		Total To Date:	

Notes:

Instructor:

Instructor's Signature:

Entry 1

Date:	Weather Conditions:
Time started:	☀ ⛅ 🌧 ⛈ 🌨
Time finished:	○ ○ ○ ○ ○
Skills Practiced:	Type of Driving (Rural, City, Highway. etc):

Day Minutes:		Night Minutes:		Total Minutes:	
Carried Forward:		Carried Forward:		Carried Forward:	
Total To Date:		Total To Date:		Total To Date:	

Notes:	Instructor:
	Instructor's Signature:

Entry 2

Date:	Weather Conditions:
Time started:	☀ ⛅ 🌧 ⛈ 🌨
Time finished:	○ ○ ○ ○ ○
Skills Practiced:	Type of Driving (Rural, City, Highway. etc):

Day Minutes:		Night Minutes:		Total Minutes:	
Carried Forward:		Carried Forward:		Carried Forward:	
Total To Date:		Total To Date:		Total To Date:	

Notes:	Instructor:
	Instructor's Signature:

Date:		Weather Conditions:

Time started:

Time finished:

Skills Practiced:

Type of Driving (Rural, City, Highway. etc):

Day Minutes:		Night Minutes:		Total Minutes:	
Carried Forward:		Carried Forward:		Carried Forward:	
Total To Date:		Total To Date:		Total To Date:	

Notes:

Instructor:

Instructor's Signature:

Date:		Weather Conditions:

Time started:

Time finished:

Skills Practiced:

Type of Driving (Rural, City, Highway. etc):

Day Minutes:		Night Minutes:		Total Minutes:	
Carried Forward:		Carried Forward:		Carried Forward:	
Total To Date:		Total To Date:		Total To Date:	

Notes:

Instructor:

Instructor's Signature:

Entry 1

📅 Date:

🕐 Time started:

🕐 Time finished:

💡 Skills Practiced:

☁ Weather Conditions:

☀ ⛅ 🌧 ⛈ 🌦
○ ○ ○ ○ ○

📍 Type of Driving (Rural,City,Highway. etc):

Day Minutes:		Night Minutes:			Total Minutes:	
Carried Forward:		Carried Forward:			Carried Forward:	
Total To Date:		Total To Date:			Total To Date:	

📝 Notes:

👤 Instructor:

🖋 Instructor's Signature:

Entry 2

📅 Date:

🕐 Time started:

🕐 Time finished:

💡 Skills Practiced:

☁ Weather Conditions:

☀ ⛅ 🌧 ⛈ 🌦
○ ○ ○ ○ ○

📍 Type of Driving (Rural,City,Highway. etc):

Day Minutes:		Night Minutes:			Total Minutes:	
Carried Forward:		Carried Forward:			Carried Forward:	
Total To Date:		Total To Date:			Total To Date:	

📝 Notes:

👤 Instructor:

🖋 Instructor's Signature:

Entry 1

Date:		Weather Conditions:

Time started:

Time finished:

Skills Practiced:

Type of Driving (Rural,City,Highway. etc):

Day Minutes:		Night Minutes:		Total Minutes:	
Carried Forward:		Carried Forward:		Carried Forward:	
Total To Date:		Total To Date:		Total To Date:	

Notes:

Instructor:

Instructor's Signature:

Entry 2

Date:		Weather Conditions:

Time started:

Time finished:

Skills Practiced:

Type of Driving (Rural,City,Highway. etc):

Day Minutes:		Night Minutes:		Total Minutes:	
Carried Forward:		Carried Forward:		Carried Forward:	
Total To Date:		Total To Date:		Total To Date:	

Notes:

Instructor:

Instructor's Signature:

Entry 1

📅 Date: _____

🕐 Time started: _____

🕐 Time finished: _____

💡 Skills Practiced:

☁ Weather Conditions:

☀ ⛅ 🌧 ⛈ 🌨
○ ○ ○ ○ ○

📍 Type of Driving (Rural, City, Highway. etc):

Day Minutes:		Night Minutes:		Total Minutes:	
Carried Forward:		Carried Forward:		Carried Forward:	
Total To Date:		Total To Date:		Total To Date:	

📝 Notes:

👤 Instructor:

🖋 Instructor's Signature:

Entry 2

📅 Date: _____

🕐 Time started: _____

🕐 Time finished: _____

💡 Skills Practiced:

☁ Weather Conditions:

☀ ⛅ 🌧 ⛈ 🌨
○ ○ ○ ○ ○

📍 Type of Driving (Rural, City, Highway. etc):

Day Minutes:		Night Minutes:		Total Minutes:	
Carried Forward:		Carried Forward:		Carried Forward:	
Total To Date:		Total To Date:		Total To Date:	

📝 Notes:

👤 Instructor:

🖋 Instructor's Signature:

Entry 1

Date:	Weather Conditions:
Time started:	☀ ⛅ 🌧 ⛈ 🌦
Time finished:	○ ○ ○ ○ ○
Skills Practiced:	Type of Driving (Rural,City,Highway. etc):

Day Minutes:		Night Minutes:		Total Minutes:	
Carried Forward:		Carried Forward:		Carried Forward:	
Total To Date:		Total To Date:		Total To Date:	

Notes:	Instructor:
	Instructor's Signature:

Entry 2

Date:	Weather Conditions:
Time started:	☀ ⛅ 🌧 ⛈ 🌦
Time finished:	○ ○ ○ ○ ○
Skills Practiced:	Type of Driving (Rural,City,Highway. etc):

Day Minutes:		Night Minutes:		Total Minutes:	
Carried Forward:		Carried Forward:		Carried Forward:	
Total To Date:		Total To Date:		Total To Date:	

Notes:	Instructor:
	Instructor's Signature:

Entry 1

Date:		
Time started:		
Time finished:		

Weather Conditions:

☀ ⛅ 🌧 ⛈ 🌧
○ ○ ○ ○ ○

Skills Practiced:

Type of Driving (Rural, City, Highway. etc):

Day Minutes:		Night Minutes:		Total Minutes:	
Carried Forward:		Carried Forward:		Carried Forward:	
Total To Date:		Total To Date:		Total To Date:	

Notes:

Instructor:

Instructor's Signature:

Entry 2

Date:		
Time started:		
Time finished:		

Weather Conditions:

☀ ⛅ 🌧 ⛈ 🌧
○ ○ ○ ○ ○

Skills Practiced:

Type of Driving (Rural, City, Highway. etc):

Day Minutes:		Night Minutes:		Total Minutes:	
Carried Forward:		Carried Forward:		Carried Forward:	
Total To Date:		Total To Date:		Total To Date:	

Notes:

Instructor:

Instructor's Signature:

Date:		Weather Conditions:

☀ 🌤 🌧 ⛈ 🌧
○   ○   ○   ○   ○

Time started:

Time finished:

Skills Practiced:

Type of Driving (Rural,City,Highway. etc):

Day Minutes:		Night Minutes:		Total Minutes:	
Carried Forward:		Carried Forward:		Carried Forward:	
Total To Date:		Total To Date:		Total To Date:	

Notes:

Instructor:

Instructor's Signature:

Date:		Weather Conditions:

☀ 🌤 🌧 ⛈ 🌧
○   ○   ○   ○   ○

Time started:

Time finished:

Skills Practiced:

Type of Driving (Rural,City,Highway. etc):

Day Minutes:		Night Minutes:		Total Minutes:	
Carried Forward:		Carried Forward:		Carried Forward:	
Total To Date:		Total To Date:		Total To Date:	

Notes:

Instructor:

Instructor's Signature:

Entry 1

Date:		Weather Conditions:	
Time started:		☀ ⛅ 🌦 ⛈ 🌧	
Time finished:		○ ○ ○ ○ ○	

Skills Practiced:

Type of Driving (Rural,City,Highway. etc):

Day Minutes:		Night Minutes:			Total Minutes:	
Carried Forward:		Carried Forward:			Carried Forward:	
Total To Date:		Total To Date:			Total To Date:	

Notes:

Instructor:

Instructor's Signature:

Entry 2

Date:		Weather Conditions:	
Time started:		☀ ⛅ 🌦 ⛈ 🌧	
Time finished:		○ ○ ○ ○ ○	

Skills Practiced:

Type of Driving (Rural,City,Highway. etc):

Day Minutes:		Night Minutes:			Total Minutes:	
Carried Forward:		Carried Forward:			Carried Forward:	
Total To Date:		Total To Date:			Total To Date:	

Notes:

Instructor:

Instructor's Signature:

📅 Date:			☁ Weather Conditions:		
🕐 Time started:					
🕐 Time finished:			☀ ⛅ 🌦 ⛈ 🌨		
💡 Skills Practiced:			📍 Type of Driving (Rural,City,Highway. etc):		

Day Minutes:		Night Minutes:		Total Minutes:	
Carried Forward:		Carried Forward:		Carried Forward:	
Total To Date:		Total To Date:		Total To Date:	

📝 Notes:	👤 Instructor:
	🖊 Instructor's Signature:

📅 Date:			☁ Weather Conditions:		
🕐 Time started:					
🕐 Time finished:			☀ ⛅ 🌦 ⛈ 🌨		
💡 Skills Practiced:			📍 Type of Driving (Rural,City,Highway. etc):		

Day Minutes:		Night Minutes:		Total Minutes:	
Carried Forward:		Carried Forward:		Carried Forward:	
Total To Date:		Total To Date:		Total To Date:	

📝 Notes:	👤 Instructor:
	🖊 Instructor's Signature:

Entry 1

📅 Date:

🕐 Time started:

🕐 Time finished:

💡 Skills Practiced:

☁ Weather Conditions:

☀ ⛅ 🌧 ⛈ 🌨
○   ○   ○   ○   ○

📍 Type of Driving (Rural,City,Highway. etc):

Day Minutes:		Night Minutes:		Total Minutes:	
Carried Forward:		Carried Forward:		Carried Forward:	
Total To Date:		Total To Date:		Total To Date:	

📝 Notes:

👤 Instructor:

✒ Instructor's Signature:

Entry 2

📅 Date:

🕐 Time started:

🕐 Time finished:

💡 Skills Practiced:

☁ Weather Conditions:

☀ ⛅ 🌧 ⛈ 🌨
○   ○   ○   ○   ○

📍 Type of Driving (Rural,City,Highway. etc):

Day Minutes:		Night Minutes:		Total Minutes:	
Carried Forward:		Carried Forward:		Carried Forward:	
Total To Date:		Total To Date:		Total To Date:	

📝 Notes:

👤 Instructor:

✒ Instructor's Signature:

📅 Date:	🗓 Weather Conditions:

🕐 Time started:	☀ 🌤 🌧 ⛈ 🌨
🕐 Time finished:	○ ○ ○ ○ ○

💡 Skills Practiced:	📍 Type of Driving (Rural,City,Highway. etc):

Day Minutes:		Night Minutes:		Total Minutes:	
Carried Forward:		Carried Forward:		Carried Forward:	
Total To Date:		Total To Date:		Total To Date:	

📝 Notes:	👤 Instructor:
	✒ Instructor's Signature:

📅 Date:	🗓 Weather Conditions:

🕐 Time started:	☀ 🌤 🌧 ⛈ 🌨
🕐 Time finished:	○ ○ ○ ○ ○

💡 Skills Practiced:	📍 Type of Driving (Rural,City,Highway. etc):

Day Minutes:		Night Minutes:		Total Minutes:	
Carried Forward:		Carried Forward:		Carried Forward:	
Total To Date:		Total To Date:		Total To Date:	

📝 Notes:	👤 Instructor:
	✒ Instructor's Signature:

📅 Date:	☁ Weather Conditions:
🕐 Time started:	☀ ⛅ 🌧 ⛈ 🌧
🕐 Time finished:	○ ○ ○ ○ ○
💡 Skills Practiced:	📍 Type of Driving (Rural,City,Highway. etc):

Day Minutes:		Night Minutes:			Total Minutes:	
Carried Forward:		Carried Forward:			Carried Forward:	
Total To Date:		Total To Date:			Total To Date:	

📝 Notes:	👤 Instructor:
	✍ Instructor's Signature:

📅 Date:	☁ Weather Conditions:
🕐 Time started:	☀ ⛅ 🌧 ⛈ 🌧
🕐 Time finished:	○ ○ ○ ○ ○
💡 Skills Practiced:	📍 Type of Driving (Rural,City,Highway. etc):

Day Minutes:		Night Minutes:			Total Minutes:	
Carried Forward:		Carried Forward:			Carried Forward:	
Total To Date:		Total To Date:			Total To Date:	

📝 Notes:	👤 Instructor:
	✍ Instructor's Signature:

Entry 1

📅 Date:		☁ Weather Conditions:
🕐 Time started:		☀ 🌤 🌧 ⛈ 🌧
🕐 Time finished:		○ ○ ○ ○ ○
💡 Skills Practiced:		📍 Type of Driving (Rural,City,Highway. etc):

Day Minutes:		Night Minutes:		Total Minutes:	
Carried Forward:		Carried Forward:		Carried Forward:	
Total To Date:		Total To Date:		Total To Date:	

📝 Notes:	👤 Instructor:
	✍ Instructor's Signature:

Entry 2

📅 Date:		☁ Weather Conditions:
🕐 Time started:		☀ 🌤 🌧 ⛈ 🌧
🕐 Time finished:		○ ○ ○ ○ ○
💡 Skills Practiced:		📍 Type of Driving (Rural,City,Highway. etc):

Day Minutes:		Night Minutes:		Total Minutes:	
Carried Forward:		Carried Forward:		Carried Forward:	
Total To Date:		Total To Date:		Total To Date:	

📝 Notes:	👤 Instructor:
	✍ Instructor's Signature:

Entry 1

📅 Date:			☁ Weather Conditions:

🕐 Time started:

🕐 Time finished:

☀ ⛅ 🌧 ⛈ 🌨
○ ○ ○ ○ ○

💡 Skills Practiced:

📍 Type of Driving (Rural, City, Highway. etc):

Day Minutes:		Night Minutes:			Total Minutes:	
Carried Forward:		Carried Forward:			Carried Forward:	
Total To Date:		Total To Date:			Total To Date:	

📝 Notes:

👤 Instructor:

🖊 Instructor's Signature:

Entry 2

📅 Date:			☁ Weather Conditions:

🕐 Time started:

🕐 Time finished:

☀ ⛅ 🌧 ⛈ 🌨
○ ○ ○ ○ ○

💡 Skills Practiced:

📍 Type of Driving (Rural, City, Highway. etc):

Day Minutes:		Night Minutes:			Total Minutes:	
Carried Forward:		Carried Forward:			Carried Forward:	
Total To Date:		Total To Date:			Total To Date:	

📝 Notes:

👤 Instructor:

🖊 Instructor's Signature:

Date:		Weather Conditions:

Time started:

Time finished:

Skills Practiced:

Type of Driving (Rural, City, Highway. etc):

Day Minutes:		Night Minutes:		Total Minutes:	
Carried Forward:		Carried Forward:		Carried Forward:	
Total To Date:		Total To Date:		Total To Date:	

Notes:

Instructor:

Instructor's Signature:

Date:		Weather Conditions:

Time started:

Time finished:

Skills Practiced:

Type of Driving (Rural, City, Highway. etc):

Day Minutes:		Night Minutes:		Total Minutes:	
Carried Forward:		Carried Forward:		Carried Forward:	
Total To Date:		Total To Date:		Total To Date:	

Notes:

Instructor:

Instructor's Signature:

Entry 1

📅 Date:		☁ Weather Conditions:				
🕐 Time started:		☀ ⛅ 🌧 ⛈ 🌨				
🕐 Time finished:		○ ○ ○ ○ ○				
💡 Skills Practiced:		📍 Type of Driving (Rural,City,Highway. etc):				

Day Minutes:		Night Minutes:		Total Minutes:	
Carried Forward:		Carried Forward:		Carried Forward:	
Total To Date:		Total To Date:		Total To Date:	

📝 Notes:	👤 Instructor:
	✍ Instructor's Signature:

Entry 2

📅 Date:		☁ Weather Conditions:				
🕐 Time started:		☀ ⛅ 🌧 ⛈ 🌨				
🕐 Time finished:		○ ○ ○ ○ ○				
💡 Skills Practiced:		📍 Type of Driving (Rural,City,Highway. etc):				

Day Minutes:		Night Minutes:		Total Minutes:	
Carried Forward:		Carried Forward:		Carried Forward:	
Total To Date:		Total To Date:		Total To Date:	

📝 Notes:	👤 Instructor:
	✍ Instructor's Signature:

Entry 1

Date:		Weather Conditions:

☀ ⛅ 🌧 ⛈ 🌦
○   ○   ○   ○   ○

Time started:
Time finished:

Skills Practiced:

Type of Driving (Rural,City,Highway. etc):

Day Minutes:		Night Minutes:		Total Minutes:	
Carried Forward:		Carried Forward:		Carried Forward:	
Total To Date:		Total To Date:		Total To Date:	

Notes:

Instructor:

Instructor's Signature:

Entry 2

Date:		Weather Conditions:

☀ ⛅ 🌧 ⛈ 🌦
○   ○   ○   ○   ○

Time started:
Time finished:

Skills Practiced:

Type of Driving (Rural,City,Highway. etc):

Day Minutes:		Night Minutes:		Total Minutes:	
Carried Forward:		Carried Forward:		Carried Forward:	
Total To Date:		Total To Date:		Total To Date:	

Notes:

Instructor:

Instructor's Signature:

📅 Date:	☁ Weather Conditions:

🕐 Time started:	
🕐 Time finished:	☀ ⛅ 🌧 ⛈ 🌧
	○　○　○　○　○

💡 Skills Practiced:	📍 Type of Driving (Rural,City,Highway. etc):

Day Minutes:		Night Minutes:			Total Minutes:	
Carried Forward:		Carried Forward:			Carried Forward:	
Total To Date:		Total To Date:			Total To Date:	

📝 Notes:	👤 Instructor:
	✒ Instructor's Signature:

📅 Date:	☁ Weather Conditions:

🕐 Time started:	
🕐 Time finished:	☀ ⛅ 🌧 ⛈ 🌧
	○　○　○　○　○

💡 Skills Practiced:	📍 Type of Driving (Rural,City,Highway. etc):

Day Minutes:		Night Minutes:			Total Minutes:	
Carried Forward:		Carried Forward:			Carried Forward:	
Total To Date:		Total To Date:			Total To Date:	

📝 Notes:	👤 Instructor:
	✒ Instructor's Signature:

Entry 1

Date:	Weather Conditions:
Time started:	☀ ⛅ 🌧 ⛈ 🌧
Time finished:	○ ○ ○ ○ ○
Skills Practiced:	Type of Driving (Rural, City, Highway. etc):

Day Minutes:		Night Minutes:		Total Minutes:	
Carried Forward:		Carried Forward:		Carried Forward:	
Total To Date:		Total To Date:		Total To Date:	

Notes:	Instructor:
	Instructor's Signature:

Entry 2

Date:	Weather Conditions:
Time started:	☀ ⛅ 🌧 ⛈ 🌧
Time finished:	○ ○ ○ ○ ○
Skills Practiced:	Type of Driving (Rural, City, Highway. etc):

Day Minutes:		Night Minutes:		Total Minutes:	
Carried Forward:		Carried Forward:		Carried Forward:	
Total To Date:		Total To Date:		Total To Date:	

Notes:	Instructor:
	Instructor's Signature:

Date:	Weather Conditions:
Time started:	☀ 🌤 🌧 ⛈ 🌦
Time finished:	○ ○ ○ ○ ○
Skills Practiced:	Type of Driving (Rural,City,Highway. etc):

Day Minutes:		Night Minutes:			Total Minutes:	
Carried Forward:		Carried Forward:			Carried Forward:	
Total To Date:		Total To Date:			Total To Date:	

Notes:	Instructor:
	Instructor's Signature:

Date:	Weather Conditions:
Time started:	☀ 🌤 🌧 ⛈ 🌦
Time finished:	○ ○ ○ ○ ○
Skills Practiced:	Type of Driving (Rural,City,Highway. etc):

Day Minutes:		Night Minutes:			Total Minutes:	
Carried Forward:		Carried Forward:			Carried Forward:	
Total To Date:		Total To Date:			Total To Date:	

Notes:	Instructor:
	Instructor's Signature:

Entry 1

📅 Date:	
🕐 Time started:	☁️ Weather Conditions:
🕐 Time finished:	☀️ ⛅ 🌧️ ⛈️ 🌨️ ○ ○ ○ ○ ○
💡 Skills Practiced:	📍 Type of Driving (Rural,City,Highway. etc):

Day Minutes:		Night Minutes:		Total Minutes:	
Carried Forward:		Carried Forward:		Carried Forward:	
Total To Date:		Total To Date:		Total To Date:	

📝 Notes:	👤 Instructor:
	✒️ Instructor's Signature:

Entry 2

📅 Date:	
🕐 Time started:	☁️ Weather Conditions:
🕐 Time finished:	☀️ ⛅ 🌧️ ⛈️ 🌨️ ○ ○ ○ ○ ○
💡 Skills Practiced:	📍 Type of Driving (Rural,City,Highway. etc):

Day Minutes:		Night Minutes:		Total Minutes:	
Carried Forward:		Carried Forward:		Carried Forward:	
Total To Date:		Total To Date:		Total To Date:	

📝 Notes:	👤 Instructor:
	✒️ Instructor's Signature:

| 📅 Date: | ☁ Weather Conditions: |

🕐 Time started:	
🕐 Time finished:	☀ ⛅ 🌧 ⛈ 🌧
	○ ○ ○ ○ ○

💡 Skills Practiced:

📍 Type of Driving (Rural,City,Highway. etc):

Day Minutes:		Night Minutes:		Total Minutes:	
Carried Forward:		Carried Forward:		Carried Forward:	
Total To Date:		Total To Date:		Total To Date:	

📝 Notes:

👤 Instructor:

✒ Instructor's Signature:

| 📅 Date: | ☁ Weather Conditions: |

🕐 Time started:	
🕐 Time finished:	☀ ⛅ 🌧 ⛈ 🌧
	○ ○ ○ ○ ○

💡 Skills Practiced:

📍 Type of Driving (Rural,City,Highway. etc):

Day Minutes:		Night Minutes:		Total Minutes:	
Carried Forward:		Carried Forward:		Carried Forward:	
Total To Date:		Total To Date:		Total To Date:	

📝 Notes:

👤 Instructor:

✒ Instructor's Signature:

Date:	Weather Conditions:
Time started:	☀ 🌤 🌧 ⛈ 🌨
Time finished:	○ ○ ○ ○ ○
Skills Practiced:	Type of Driving (Rural, City, Highway. etc):

Day Minutes:		Night Minutes:		Total Minutes:	
Carried Forward:		Carried Forward:		Carried Forward:	
Total To Date:		Total To Date:		Total To Date:	

Notes:	Instructor:
	Instructor's Signature:

Date:	Weather Conditions:
Time started:	☀ 🌤 🌧 ⛈ 🌨
Time finished:	○ ○ ○ ○ ○
Skills Practiced:	Type of Driving (Rural, City, Highway. etc):

Day Minutes:		Night Minutes:		Total Minutes:	
Carried Forward:		Carried Forward:		Carried Forward:	
Total To Date:		Total To Date:		Total To Date:	

Notes:	Instructor:
	Instructor's Signature:

Entry 1

📅 Date:		☁️ Weather Conditions:	
🕐 Time started:		☀️ ⛅ 🌧️ ⛈️ 🌧️	
🕐 Time finished:		○ ○ ○ ○ ○	
💡 Skills Practiced:		📍 Type of Driving (Rural,City,Highway. etc):	

Day Minutes:		Night Minutes:			Total Minutes:	
Carried Forward:		Carried Forward:			Carried Forward:	
Total To Date:		Total To Date:			Total To Date:	

📝 Notes:	👤 Instructor:
	✒️ Instructor's Signature:

Entry 2

📅 Date:		☁️ Weather Conditions:	
🕐 Time started:		☀️ ⛅ 🌧️ ⛈️ 🌧️	
🕐 Time finished:		○ ○ ○ ○ ○	
💡 Skills Practiced:		📍 Type of Driving (Rural,City,Highway. etc):	

Day Minutes:		Night Minutes:			Total Minutes:	
Carried Forward:		Carried Forward:			Carried Forward:	
Total To Date:		Total To Date:			Total To Date:	

📝 Notes:	👤 Instructor:
	✒️ Instructor's Signature:

📅 Date:		☁ Weather Conditions:		
🕐 Time started:				
🕐 Time finished:		☀ ⛅ 🌧 ⛈ 🌧 ◯ ◯ ◯ ◯ ◯		
💡 Skills Practiced:		📍 Type of Driving (Rural,City,Highway. etc):		

Day Minutes:		Night Minutes:			Total Minutes:	
Carried Forward:		Carried Forward:			Carried Forward:	
Total To Date:		Total To Date:			Total To Date:	

📝 Notes:	👤 Instructor:
	✒ Instructor's Signature:

📅 Date:		☁ Weather Conditions:		
🕐 Time started:				
🕐 Time finished:		☀ ⛅ 🌧 ⛈ 🌧 ◯ ◯ ◯ ◯ ◯		
💡 Skills Practiced:		📍 Type of Driving (Rural,City,Highway. etc):		

Day Minutes:		Night Minutes:			Total Minutes:	
Carried Forward:		Carried Forward:			Carried Forward:	
Total To Date:		Total To Date:			Total To Date:	

📝 Notes:	👤 Instructor:
	✒ Instructor's Signature:

Entry 1

📅 Date:				
🕐 Time started:				
🕐 Time finished:				

☁ Weather Conditions:

☀ ⛅ 🌧 ⛈ 🌦
○　○　○　○　○

💡 Skills Practiced:

📍 Type of Driving (Rural,City,Highway. etc):

Day Minutes:		Night Minutes:		Total Minutes:	
Carried Forward:		Carried Forward:		Carried Forward:	
Total To Date:		Total To Date:		Total To Date:	

📝 Notes:

👤 Instructor:

🖋 Instructor's Signature:

Entry 2

📅 Date:				
🕐 Time started:				
🕐 Time finished:				

☁ Weather Conditions:

☀ ⛅ 🌧 ⛈ 🌦
○　○　○　○　○

💡 Skills Practiced:

📍 Type of Driving (Rural,City,Highway. etc):

Day Minutes:		Night Minutes:		Total Minutes:	
Carried Forward:		Carried Forward:		Carried Forward:	
Total To Date:		Total To Date:		Total To Date:	

📝 Notes:

👤 Instructor:

🖋 Instructor's Signature:

⊞ Date:				☁ Weather Conditions:			
🕐 Time started:				☀ ⛅ 🌧 ⛈ 🌨			
🕐 Time finished:				○ ○ ○ ○ ○			
💡 Skills Practiced:				📍 Type of Driving (Rural,City,Highway. etc):			

Day Minutes:		Night Minutes:			Total Minutes:	
Carried Forward:		Carried Forward:			Carried Forward:	
Total To Date:		Total To Date:			Total To Date:	

📝 Notes:	👤 Instructor:
	🖋 Instructor's Signature:

⊞ Date:				☁ Weather Conditions:			
🕐 Time started:				☀ ⛅ 🌧 ⛈ 🌨			
🕐 Time finished:				○ ○ ○ ○ ○			
💡 Skills Practiced:				📍 Type of Driving (Rural,City,Highway. etc):			

Day Minutes:		Night Minutes:			Total Minutes:	
Carried Forward:		Carried Forward:			Carried Forward:	
Total To Date:		Total To Date:			Total To Date:	

📝 Notes:	👤 Instructor:
	🖋 Instructor's Signature:

📅 Date: _____

🕐 Time started: _____

🕐 Time finished: _____

🔆 Skills Practiced:

☁ Weather Conditions:

☀ ⛅ 🌧 ⛈ 🌨
○ ○ ○ ○ ○

📍 Type of Driving (Rural,City,Highway. etc):

Day Minutes:		Night Minutes:		Total Minutes:	
Carried Forward:		Carried Forward:		Carried Forward:	
Total To Date:		Total To Date:		Total To Date:	

📝 Notes:

👤 Instructor:

✍ Instructor's Signature:

📅 Date: _____

🕐 Time started: _____

🕐 Time finished: _____

🔆 Skills Practiced:

☁ Weather Conditions:

☀ ⛅ 🌧 ⛈ 🌨
○ ○ ○ ○ ○

📍 Type of Driving (Rural,City,Highway. etc):

Day Minutes:		Night Minutes:		Total Minutes:	
Carried Forward:		Carried Forward:		Carried Forward:	
Total To Date:		Total To Date:		Total To Date:	

📝 Notes:

👤 Instructor:

✍ Instructor's Signature:

Entry 1

📅 Date: _____

🕐 Time started: _____

🕐 Time finished: _____

☁ Weather Conditions:

☀ ◯   ⛅ ◯   🌧 ◯   ⛈ ◯   🌧 ◯

🔆 Skills Practiced:

📍 Type of Driving (Rural, City, Highway. etc):

Day Minutes:		Night Minutes:		Total Minutes:	
Carried Forward:		Carried Forward:		Carried Forward:	
Total To Date:		Total To Date:		Total To Date:	

📝 Notes:

👤 Instructor:

🖋 Instructor's Signature:

Entry 2

📅 Date: _____

🕐 Time started: _____

🕐 Time finished: _____

☁ Weather Conditions:

☀ ◯   ⛅ ◯   🌧 ◯   ⛈ ◯   🌧 ◯

🔆 Skills Practiced:

📍 Type of Driving (Rural, City, Highway. etc):

Day Minutes:		Night Minutes:		Total Minutes:	
Carried Forward:		Carried Forward:		Carried Forward:	
Total To Date:		Total To Date:		Total To Date:	

📝 Notes:

👤 Instructor:

🖋 Instructor's Signature:

Entry 1

📅 Date:

🕐 Time started:

🕐 Time finished:

💡 Skills Practiced:

☁ Weather Conditions:

☀ ⛅ 🌧 ⛈ 🌨
○ ○ ○ ○ ○

📍 Type of Driving (Rural, City, Highway. etc):

Day Minutes:		Night Minutes:		Total Minutes:	
Carried Forward:		Carried Forward:		Carried Forward:	
Total To Date:		Total To Date:		Total To Date:	

📝 Notes:

👤 Instructor:

🖊 Instructor's Signature:

Entry 2

📅 Date:

🕐 Time started:

🕐 Time finished:

💡 Skills Practiced:

☁ Weather Conditions:

☀ ⛅ 🌧 ⛈ 🌨
○ ○ ○ ○ ○

📍 Type of Driving (Rural, City, Highway. etc):

Day Minutes:		Night Minutes:		Total Minutes:	
Carried Forward:		Carried Forward:		Carried Forward:	
Total To Date:		Total To Date:		Total To Date:	

📝 Notes:

👤 Instructor:

🖊 Instructor's Signature:

Date:	Weather Conditions:
Time started:	☀ ⛅ ☁ ⛈ ☁
Time finished:	○ ○ ○ ○ ○
Skills Practiced:	Type of Driving (Rural,City,Highway. etc):

Day Minutes:		Night Minutes:			Total Minutes:	
Carried Forward:		Carried Forward:			Carried Forward:	
Total To Date:		Total To Date:			Total To Date:	

Notes:	Instructor:
	Instructor's Signature:

Date:	Weather Conditions:
Time started:	☀ ⛅ ☁ ⛈ ☁
Time finished:	○ ○ ○ ○ ○
Skills Practiced:	Type of Driving (Rural,City,Highway. etc):

Day Minutes:		Night Minutes:			Total Minutes:	
Carried Forward:		Carried Forward:			Carried Forward:	
Total To Date:		Total To Date:			Total To Date:	

Notes:	Instructor:
	Instructor's Signature:

Date:	Weather Conditions:
Time started:	☀ ⛅ 🌧 ⛈ 🌧
Time finished:	○ ○ ○ ○ ○
Skills Practiced:	Type of Driving (Rural,City,Highway. etc):

Day Minutes:		Night Minutes:			Total Minutes:	
Carried Forward:		Carried Forward:			Carried Forward:	
Total To Date:		Total To Date:			Total To Date:	

Notes:	Instructor:
	Instructor's Signature:

Date:	Weather Conditions:
Time started:	☀ ⛅ 🌧 ⛈ 🌧
Time finished:	○ ○ ○ ○ ○
Skills Practiced:	Type of Driving (Rural,City,Highway. etc):

Day Minutes:		Night Minutes:			Total Minutes:	
Carried Forward:		Carried Forward:			Carried Forward:	
Total To Date:		Total To Date:			Total To Date:	

Notes:	Instructor:
	Instructor's Signature:

📅 Date:	☁ Weather Conditions:

🕐 Time started:	☀ ⛅ 🌧 ⛈ 🌨
🕐 Time finished:	○ ○ ○ ○ ○

🔆 Skills Practiced:	📍 Type of Driving (Rural,City,Highway. etc):

Day Minutes:		Night Minutes:		Total Minutes:	
Carried Forward:		Carried Forward:		Carried Forward:	
Total To Date:		Total To Date:		Total To Date:	

📝 Notes:	👤 Instructor:
	✍ Instructor's Signature:

📅 Date:	☁ Weather Conditions:

🕐 Time started:	☀ ⛅ 🌧 ⛈ 🌨
🕐 Time finished:	○ ○ ○ ○ ○

🔆 Skills Practiced:	📍 Type of Driving (Rural,City,Highway. etc):

Day Minutes:		Night Minutes:		Total Minutes:	
Carried Forward:		Carried Forward:		Carried Forward:	
Total To Date:		Total To Date:		Total To Date:	

📝 Notes:	👤 Instructor:
	✍ Instructor's Signature:

Made in the USA
Columbia, SC
15 June 2022